Django

Django Framework Mastery - Crafting Professional-Grade Web Solutions

Jax Montgomery

Table of Contents

Introduction
Setting the stage for mastering Django and building professional-grade web solutions

In the dynamic realm of modern web development, mastering a framework that seamlessly blends elegance, efficiency, and scalability is paramount. Enter Django, a high-level Python web framework that empowers developers to craft professional-grade web solutions with precision and finesse. In this foundational chapter, we embark on a journey to understand the pivotal role of Django in the web development landscape and lay the groundwork for achieving mastery in this versatile framework.

Understanding the Importance of Architecture in Web Development

Web improvement is now not restricted to inactive pages and basic shapes. As computerized encounters ended up more complex and intelligently, the require for well-structured and effective design has heightens. A strong engineering not as it were improves practicality and extensibility but too contributes essentially to the by and large execution of web applications.

Django, being a framework that adheres to the "Don't Repeat Yourself" (DRY) principle, facilitates the creation of organized and structured codebases. This enables developers to focus on creating feature-rich applications without getting entangled in redundant and cumbersome code.

Let's illustrate the significance of architecture with a simplified example:

python

```python
# Without proper architecture
def calculate_tax(income):
    # ... complex tax calculation logic ...
    return tax_amount

def generate_invoice(customer, items):
    # ... complex invoice generation logic ...
    return invoice

# With proper architecture
class TaxCalculator:
    def calculate_tax(self, income):
        # ... complex tax calculation logic ...
        return tax_amount

class InvoiceGenerator:
    def generate_invoice(self, customer, items):
        # ... complex invoice generation logic ...
        return invoice
```

In the latter example, we've embraced a more structured approach, encapsulating related functionalities within separate classes. Django takes this concept to heart by promoting the use of reusable apps, modular project structures, and clear separation of concerns.

Setting Up for Success: Laying the Foundation

Before embarking on the journey of crafting professional-grade web solutions with Django, it's imperative to establish an optimal development environment. This includes setting up Python, a virtual environment, and installing Django itself. Here's a glimpse of the initial steps:

1. Install Python: Guarantee you have got Python installed on your machine. Django is compatible with Python 3.6 or higher. You'll confirm your Python adaptation by running python --form in your terminal.

2. Create a Virtual Environment: Virtual environments isolate project dependencies, preventing conflicts with system-wide packages. Create a new virtual environment by executing:

```
python -m venv myenv
```

3. Activate the Virtual Environment: Activate the virtual environment using the appropriate command for your operating system:

   - On Windows: myenv\Scripts\activate
   - On macOS and Linux: source myenv/bin/activate
4. Install Django: With the virtual environment activated, install Django using pip:

```
pip install django
```

5. Verify Installation: Confirm the successful installation of Django by running django-admin --version.

Exploring the Django Project Structure

Django follows a well-defined project structure that facilitates organization and maintainability. As you progress toward mastering Django, it's essential to become familiar with this structure.

A typical Django project is organized as follows:

markdown

```
project_name/
├── manage.py
├── project_name/
│   ├── __init__.py
│   ├── settings.py
│   ├── urls.py
│   └── wsgi.py
└── app_name/
    ├── migrations/
    ├── __init__.py
    ├── admin.py
    ├── models.py
    ├── views.py
    └── ...
```

- manage.py: A command-line utility to interact with the project.
- project_name/: The project's container.
  - settings.py: Configuration settings for the project.
  - urls.py: URL routing configuration.

- o   wsgi.py: WSGI application entry point.
- app_name/: A modular component of the project, representing a specific application or feature.
  - o   migrations/: Database schema evolution history.
  - o   admin.py: Admin interface configuration.
  - o   models.py: Data models definition.
  - o   views.py: View functions handling HTTP requests.

As we set out on the travel to acing Django and making professional-grade web arrangements, we've laid the foundation by understanding the significance of design in cutting edge web improvement. Django's commitment to clean code, division of concerns, and seclusion gives a strong establishment for building vigorous and versatile applications.

Within the another chapter, we'll dig into the progressed viewpoints of extend setup and structure, investigating procedures to organize huge Django ventures, actualize a measured design, and design settings for different sending situations. By mastering these basics, you will be prepared to promote your Django expertise and set out on the creation of advanced, high-quality web arrangements that sparkle within the advanced scene.

Understanding the importance of architecture in web development

Within the ever-changing domain of web improvement, the part of structural plan cannot be overstated. Engineering gives the basic system for building solid, adaptable, and feasible web applications. A well-structured engineering not as it were streamlines advancement endeavors but too contributes to the in general execution and solidness of the computer program.

1. Architecture as the Blueprint of a Web Application:

Within the setting of web development, engineering alludes to the high-level plan and organization of a web application. It envelops the course of action of components, modules, and designs that shape the building pieces of the application. A strong engineering plan offers a clear diagram for designers to take after, directing them in making an application that fulfills its destinations productively.

2. Benefits of a Solid Architectural Design:

a. Scalability: An architectural design that accommodates growth and expansion is vital for web applications. Scalability ensures that the application can handle increasing user loads and data volumes without compromising performance. By adhering to principles like modularization and loose coupling, an application can scale seamlessly to meet future demands.

b. Maintainability: A well-structured architecture simplifies maintenance and updates to the application. When components are logically separated and organized, developers can quickly locate and modify specific functionalities without impacting other parts of the system. This reduces the risk of introducing unintended bugs during maintenance.

c. Security: Architecture plays a significant part in guaranteeing the security of a web application. A well-designed engineering permits for the usage of security measures at different levels, such as input approval, confirmation, and get to control. A vigorous design makes a difference watch against common security vulnerabilities, such as SQL infusion and cross-site scripting (XSS).

d. Code Reusability: A good architectural design promotes the creation of reusable components. Reusable code reduces duplication and improves consistency across the application. Developers can leverage existing components in new features, saving development time and effort.

3. Key Architectural Patterns in Web Development:

a. Model-View-Controller (MVC): MVC is one of the foremost predominant engineering designs in web advancement. It isolates the application into three unmistakable components:

Demonstrate (information and trade rationale), View (client interface), and Controller (mediator that handles client input and overhauls the demonstrate and see). The MVC design advances code organization and division of concerns, empowering less demanding upkeep and testing.

python

```python
# Example of a simple Django view using the MVC pattern
from django.shortcuts import render
from django.http import HttpResponse
from .models import BlogPost

def blog_post_list(request):
    posts = BlogPost.objects.all()
    return render(request, 'blog_post_list.html',
{'posts': posts})
```

b. Microservices Architecture: In this pattern, a web application is broken down into small, independent services that can be developed, deployed, and maintained separately. Each service handles a specific business function and communicates with others through APIs. Microservices promote agility and scalability, making it easier to update and scale individual components of the application.

c. Event-Driven Architecture (EDA): EDA is based on the concept of events, where components communicate by emitting and reacting to events. Events represent significant occurrences in the system and can trigger actions in other components. EDA allows for the decoupling of services and fosters real-time responsiveness.

python

```python
# Example of event-driven communication using Django
signals
from django.db.models.signals import post_save
from django.dispatch import receiver
from .models import Order

@receiver(post_save, sender=Order)
def order_created(sender, instance, **kwargs):
    # Code to handle order creation event
    pass
```

4. Selecting the Right Architecture:

Choosing the appropriate architectural pattern depends on various factors, including the application's requirements, team expertise, and future growth plans. While MVC is widely used for its simplicity and versatility, microservices and event-driven architecture are preferred for complex and highly scalable systems.

In conclusion, recognizing the centrality of design in web improvement is fundamental for building effective, strong, and versatile web applications. A well-designed building establishment cultivates versatility, practicality, security, and code reusability. By selecting the correct structural design for a particular venture, engineers can guarantee that the application is well-prepared to meet the challenges of the energetic web **development landscape.**

Chapter One

Advanced Project Setup and Structure
Organizing large Django projects with reusable apps

In the ever-changing landscape of contemporary web development, the value of a well-ordered codebase cannot be overstated. Handling extensive Django projects necessitates meticulous architectural planning to ensure manageability, scalability, and seamless collaboration among development teams. One of the keystones to achieving effective project organization revolves around the strategic utilization of reusable applications. This chapter delves into the intricate art of structuring substantial Django projects by harnessing the prowess of reusable applications, empowering developers to craft modular, effective, and adaptable solutions.

Grasping the Essence of Reusability:

Reusable applications are autonomous components that encapsulate particular functionalities, modules, or features within a Django project. These applications are meticulously designed to be autonomous, promoting modularity and isolation while encouraging synergy across various aspects of the application. Adhering to the "Don't Repeat Yourself" (DRY) philosophy, reusable applications eliminate superfluous code repetition, enhance maintainability, and expedite the development cycle.

Advantages of Reusable Applications:

1. Modularity: Reusable applications compartmentalize functionalities, enabling developers to focus on specific features without the burden of unrelated code. Each application can be developed, tested, and maintained independently, resulting in code that is more refined and succinct.

2. Collaboration: In extensive projects involving multiple developers, reusable applications facilitate seamless collaboration by delineating clear boundaries for code ownership. Various teams can concurrently work on distinct applications, reducing conflicts and streamlining the development process.

3. Scalability: As projects mature, the ability to scale distinct features becomes indispensable. Reusable applications can be expanded, refined, or even replaced with updated versions, all while preserving the core functionality of the application.

4. Maintainability: Isolating different components into applications simplifies maintenance. Updates or bug fixes can be applied to a single application without impacting the entirety of the project, minimizing the likelihood of unintended complications.

Crafting Reusable Applications:

Constructing a reusable application follows the conventional structure of a Django application, with additional considerations for reusability. Here's a stepwise guide to creating a reusable application:

1. Application Structure: Design the application with a well-defined directory structure. Integrate a README document for documentation, a setup.py file for packaging purposes, and an app_name/ directory housing the application's codebase.

2. Dependencies: Explicitly specify any external dependencies in the setup.py file to ensure effortless installation of the application in diverse projects.

3. Testing: Devote time to crafting comprehensive unit and integration tests to guarantee the flawless operation of the application. The practice of continuous integration can further elevate the dependability of your reusable application.

4. Documentation: Present lucid and concise documentation encompassing installation instructions, illustrative usage scenarios, and any available configuration choices.

Leveraging Reusable Applications:

Integrating a reusable application into your Django project involves a straightforward process:

1. Installation: Incorporate the application into your project's virtual environment using the pip package manager:

bash

```
pip install your-reusable-application
```

2. Configuration: Append the application's name to the INSTALLED_APPS list in your project's settings file:

python

```
# settings.py
INSTALLED_APPS = [
    # ...
    'your_reusable_application',
]
```

3. Application: Access the application's functionality by importing its constituents into your project's codebase:

python

```
# views.py
from your_reusable_application.models import CustomModel
```

Concrete Example:

Imagine developing an e-commerce platform with discrete modules encompassing user authentication, product catalog management, and payment processing. By fabricating reusable applications for each of these modules, you guarantee that they can be seamlessly integrated across diverse projects sans code replication. Modifications and enhancements to these modules can be executed individually, ameliorating the overall maintainability and scalability of the application.

To conclude, the art of harmonizing complex Django projects through reusable applications is an indispensable skill for contemporary web developers. By embracing the principles of modularity and adhering to established best practices, developers can harness the potency of reusable applications to streamline development processes, heighten collaborative endeavors, and construct web solutions that are both efficient and adaptable. Reusable applications underscore a fundamental stride toward attaining a methodically structured codebase that not only simplifies development but also lays the groundwork for forthcoming growth and innovation.

Implementing a modular and scalable project structure

In the contemporary realm of web development, constructing intricate and expansive applications necessitates a strategic approach to project structure. An intelligently devised project framework serves as the blueprint for creating applications that are both maintainable and scalable. This chapter delves into the art of designing a modular and adaptable project structure, revealing methodologies that empower developers to navigate the complexities of large-scale projects with precision and effectiveness.

The Importance of Project Framework:

The project framework is more than a cosmetic choice; it influences the organization and flow of a Django application. A modular and adaptable project structure is vital to address the challenges posed by changing requirements, diverse team dynamics, and the ever-evolving technological landscape.

Modularity at the Heart of Project Structure:

A modular project structure involves the division of a Django application into distinct, self-contained components known as modules or apps. Each app represents a specific functionality or feature, encapsulating related models, views, templates, and other components. This division ensures that developers can concentrate on specific parts of the application without being entangled in unrelated code.

Benefits of Modularity:

1. Isolation: Modularity guarantees that each app operates independently. This isolation minimizes the possibility of one section of the application affecting the functionality of another, enhancing the overall reliability and robustness.

2. Collaboration: Different teams or developers can work on separate apps simultaneously, promoting collaboration while mitigating conflicts that may arise from shared components.

3. Reusability: Modular apps are engineered for reusability. They can be seamlessly integrated into multiple projects, conserving development time and ensuring code consistency.

Developing a Modular Django App:

Let's outline the steps for creating a modular Django app:

1. App Structure: Within your project, initiate a new app using the command:

bash

```
python manage.py startapp app_name
```

2. Organize Components: Arrange your app's components into directories such as models/, views/, templates/, and more. This systematic organization enhances clarity and ease of maintenance.

3. Autonomy: Craft the app to be self-sustained. Avoid tight interdependencies with other apps to preserve the essence of modularity.

Scalability Infused into Project Structure:

Scalability involves conceptualizing a project structure that is primed for future growth and evolution. As an application evolves, the project structure should seamlessly accommodate new features, adapt to evolving requirements, and seamlessly handle increased user traffic.

Structural Approaches for Scalability:

1. Microservices Architecture: In this approach, the application is divided into small, self-contained services that can be independently developed, deployed, and scaled. This promotes agility and responsiveness to changes.

2. Service-Oriented Architecture (SOA): SOA revolves around the concept of autonomous services communicating via APIs. Each service corresponds to a specific business function and can be individually developed and scaled.

Illustration of Microservices Approach:

python

```
# Project structure for a microservices-based Django
application
project_name/
```

```
├── user_service/
│   ├── models.py
│   ├── views.py
│   └── ...
├── catalog_service/
│   ├── models.py
│   ├── views.py
│   └── ...
├── payment_service/
│   ├── models.py
│   ├── views.py
│   └── ...
├── ...
```

Guidelines for Implementing Scalability:

1. Decoupling: Foster loose coupling between components to facilitate seamless replacement or enhancement without causing disruptions.

2. Horizontal Scaling: Construct components to scale horizontally by adding more instances or servers. Incorporating load balancing strategies aids in distributing user requests.

3. Database Sharding: Distribute data across multiple databases or servers to prevent database bottlenecks and augment overall performance.

In summary, weaving a modular and adaptable project framework in Django is a pivotal skill in constructing applications that can adeptly accommodate changes, growth, and collaborative development. A well-structured project framework supports modularity, enabling teams to work efficiently on distinct aspects. Simultaneously, an adaptable structure assures that the application can gracefully handle expanding demands and evolving functionalities. By mastering the finesse of project framework, developers position themselves to construct web solutions that are resilient, future-proof, and well-equipped to flourish in the dynamic landscape of modern web development.

Configuring settings for different deployment environments

Within the intricate sphere of web application deployment, adaptability and fluidity reign supreme. The seamless transition of a web application across diverse deployment environments, including development, testing, and production, while preserving consistent behavior and optimal performance, is a pivotal pursuit. This chapter delves into the integral discipline of configuring settings for distinct deployment contexts in Django. This crucial skill empowers developers to adeptly manage varied deployment scenarios and maintain an elevated level of authority over the application's conduct.

Significance of Deployment Context Configuration:

The assorted contexts of web application deployment inherently carry distinct requisites. Development environments prioritize attributes like comprehensive error reporting and debugging utilities, while production environments emphasize stability, security, and performance. The mastery of deploying environment configuration empowers developers to calibrate application behavior to each context, all the while sidestepping alterations to the core codebase.

Elegance of Concern Segregation:

The design philosophy of concern segregation, deeply embedded within Django's architecture, extends gracefully to deployment environment configuration. The crux of this approach entails partitioning the settings.py file, a central repository for application configuration, into multiple entities, each devoted to a specific deployment environment. This modular strategy imparts a streamlined maintenance trajectory, minimizes errors, and amplifies the overall development workflow.

Maneuvering Through Deployment Contexts:

The conceptual landscape of Django boasts the utilization of the DJANGO_SETTINGS_MODULE environment variable, which elegantly discerns the intended settings module to be invoked. This variable assumes the Python path of the selected settings module, which usually materializes as a Python module featuring configurations germane to a distinct deployment context.

Hierarchy of Configuration:

1. Unified Settings: Commingle settings universally pertinent across all deployment environments within

the settings_common.py module. This designated haven accommodates configurations that maintain their uniformity, regardless of the particular deployment context.

2. Environment-Centric Settings: Institute independent settings modules tailored for each deployment context, such as settings_development.py, settings_testing.py, and settings_production.py. These bespoke enclaves inherit the core of their attributes from settings_common.py while affording the liberty to either augment or override configurations to match specific necessities.

3. Harnessing the Settings: Set the DJANGO_SETTINGS_MODULE environment variable to synch with the desired settings module. For instance, to engage development settings, execute:

bash

```
export
DJANGO_SETTINGS_MODULE=myproject.settings_development
```

Customized Configuration Overrides:

Every deployment context may demand nuanced configurations, deviating from the default norms. For instance, debugging tools like the Django Debug Toolbar could be indispensable in the development realm, while their relevance might wane in production to bolster performance.

Exemplar of Development Settings Refinement:

python

```
# settings development.py
from .settings_common import *

DEBUG = True
INSTALLED_APPS += ['debug_toolbar']
```

Harvesting the Bounty of Configuration Management Tools:

The arsenal of configuration management tools, including but not limited to environment variables and configuration files, bequeaths an additional layer of prowess to deployment environment configuration. These tools advocate for external modifications of settings sans any need to meddle with the sacred codebase.

Realm of Environment Variables:

Environment variables operate as conduits for runtime configuration value assignment. For instance, the SECRET_KEY environment variable can seamlessly govern the secret key earmarked for encryption purposes.

bash

```
export SECRET_KEY=mysecretkey
```

Spectrum of Configuration Files:

External configuration files prove invaluable in the dynamic orchestration of settings. Formats like YAML or JSON are revered choices. This approach acts as a bulwark, segregating sensitive data such as database credentials from the core codebase.

The virtuosity of configuring settings for distinct deployment environments resonates as a cornerstone of sagacious web application deployment. By orchestrating settings modules with finesse, orchestrating custom overrides, and harnessing the might of configuration management tools, developers galvanize the application's behavior in tune with divergent contexts. This heightened level of adaptability not only elevates the maintainability quotient but also coalesces into the creation of applications characterized by robustness and adaptability, flourishing seamlessly across diverse deployment canvases.

Chapter Two

Customizing the Django Admin Interface

Extending the admin interface with custom views and components

In the vibrant realm of web development, the creation of top-tier applications encompasses more than just features; it entails delivering a seamless and captivating user journey. Django, renowned for its adaptability and efficiency, doesn't merely enable the construction of potent backend systems but also empowers developers to design intuitive, tailored, and customizable user interfaces. This chapter embarks on the voyage of extending the Django admin interface by infusing it with bespoke views and components, thus magnifying your capacity to provide bespoke, user-friendly administrative encounters.

The Virtues of Tailoring:

The Django admin interface functions as a central hub for data and configuration management. While the default admin interface offers essential utilities, the ability to personalize it allows you to orchestrate the user experience in alignment with your application's distinct demands. By embedding custom views and components, you can introduce fresh functionalities, data visualizations, and refined workflows that harmonize perfectly with your application's requisites.

Foraying into Custom Admin Views:

Django's admin interface is constructed using Django's views, which seamlessly facilitates the incorporation of your unique views. These views can display information from your application's models, interact with external APIs, or offer analytics through a user-friendly lens.

Illustration: Forging a Custom Admin View:

python

```python
# admin.py
from django.contrib import admin
from .models import Product

@admin.register(Product)
class ProductAdmin(admin.ModelAdmin):
    list_display = ('name', 'price', 'stock')
    actions = ['increase_price']

    def increase_price(self, request, queryset):
        # Custom logic for raising prices of selected products
        pass
    increase_price.short_description = "Elevate Prices"
```

In the instance above, a custom admin view for the Product model is crafted. Data display is customized, and a custom action, "Elevate Prices," is introduced for selected products.

Embedding Bespoke Admin Components:

To enhance user experiences further, custom components can be woven into the admin interface. These components might entail advanced data visualizations, interactive graphs, or dynamic widgets that furnish real-time insights to administrators.

Demonstration: Weaving in a Tailored Chart Component:

python

```python
# admin.py
from django.contrib import admin
from .models import SalesData
from django_admin_listfilter_dropdown.filters import DropdownFilter

@admin.register(SalesData)
class SalesDataAdmin(admin.ModelAdmin):
    list_display = ('date', 'total_sales')
    list_filter = (('date', DropdownFilter),)
    change_list_template =
'admin/salesdata_change_list.html'
```

In this scenario, a personalized chart component is integrated to visualize sales data's temporal progression. The django_admin_listfilter_dropdown package bolsters filtering options within the admin interface.

Enhancing the User Experience:

When expanding the admin interface with customized views and components, consider these best practices:

1. User-Friendly Design: Design custom views and components with user-friendliness at the forefront. User interaction and comprehension of the added functionalities are pivotal.

2. Performance Optimization: Streamline the performance of bespoke components to forestall any lag in the admin interface. Utilize caching and resourceful data retrieval strategies as needed.

3. Security Assurance: Integrate apt authorization checks and access controls for custom views and components to uphold data security.

4. Thorough Documentation: Furnish administrators with lucid documentation on using the custom views and components incorporated into the admin interface.

The expansion of the Django admin interface through personalized views and components proves a potent tactic in elevating user experiences within your applications. The crafting of exclusive views, the introduction of custom actions, and the interweaving of interactive components not only enhance the admin interface's utility but also underscore your adeptness in sculpting high-caliber web solutions that excel both in backend robustness and frontend user engagement.

Implementing advanced data visualization in the admin dashboard

In the ever-evolving realm of web development, the admin dashboard takes center stage as a pivotal hub for managing and overseeing applications. As technological boundaries expand, the ability to convey intricate data insights swiftly and intuitively has become paramount. Django, a dynamic framework renowned for its adaptability, not only empowers developers to manage data but also provides the capacity to present it in an impactful visual format. Within this chapter, we embark on the journey of implementing advanced data visualization within the admin dashboard, augmenting your capability to present data-driven insights with efficacy and flair.

The Evolution of Data Display:

While the default Django admin dashboard caters to essential data management needs, the infusion of advanced data visualization introduces a transformative dimension. Effective data visualization distills intricate information into easily digestible formats, enabling administrators to swiftly arrive at informed decisions. By embedding interactive graphs, charts, and visual elements, developers enhance the admin dashboard's utility, transforming it into a potent instrument for monitoring application trends and performance metrics.

Selecting the Right Visualization Tools:

The Django developer's toolkit offers an array of data visualization libraries. Choices such as Matplotlib, Plotly, and Chart.js present diverse options for creating various chart types, spanning simple line graphs to intricate heatmaps. The selection of the ideal library hinges on factors such as data complexity, desired visual representation, and the level of interactivity sought.

Illustration: Integrating Matplotlib for Line Graphs:

python

```python
# admin.py
from django.contrib import admin
from .models import SalesData
import matplotlib.pyplot as plt
import io
import base64

@admin.register(SalesData)
class SalesDataAdmin(admin.ModelAdmin):
    list_display = ('date', 'total_sales',
'visualize_sales')

    def visualize_sales(self, obj):
        # Generating and rendering a line chart using
Matplotlib
        plt.figure(figsize=(8, 6))
        plt.plot(obj.dates, obj.sales)
        plt.title('Sales Data Visualization')
        plt.xlabel('Date')
        plt.ylabel('Sales')
        plt.grid()

        # Saving the chart to a buffer
        buffer = io.BytesIO()
        plt.savefig(buffer, format='png')
        buffer.seek(0)

        # Encoding the chart image to base64
```

```
        image_base64 =
base64.b64encode(buffer.read()).decode('utf-8')

        # Displaying the chart image in the admin
interface
        return f'<img
src="data:image/png;base64,{image_base64}"
width="400"/>'
    visualize_sales.short_description = 'Sales Chart'
```

In the scenario above, the visualize_sales method crafts a line chart using Matplotlib. The chart image is encoded in base64 and presented within the admin dashboard for each SalesData instance.

Interactive Dashboards with Plotly:

For applications demanding interactive dashboards, Plotly proves an excellent choice. Plotly facilitates the creation of interactive charts such as scatter plots, bar graphs, and heatmaps equipped with zoom, pan, and hover functionalities. These interactive elements empower administrators to delve deep into data trends and patterns.

Illustration: Formulating an Interactive Bar Graph with Plotly:

python

```
# admin.py
from django.contrib import admin
from .models import Product
import plotly.express as px

@admin.register(Product)
class ProductAdmin(admin.ModelAdmin):
```

```
    list_display = ('name', 'price', 'inventory',
'visualize_inventory')

    def visualize_inventory(self, obj):
        # Creating an interactive bar graph using
Plotly
        fig = px.bar(
            x=obj.categories,
            y=obj.inventory,
            title='Product Inventory Visualization',
            labels={'x': 'Categories', 'y':
'Inventory'},
        )
        fig.update_layout(showlegend=False)
        return fig.to_html()
    visualize_inventory.short_description = 'Inventory
Graph'
```

In this instance, the visualize_inventory method crafts an interactive bar graph using Plotly. The graph is embedded as HTML within the admin dashboard.

Prioritizing User-Friendly Interaction:

When implementing advanced data visualization within the admin dashboard, bear in mind these guiding principles:

1. **Relevance**: Choose visualizations closely aligned with the intended data insights.
2. **Interactivity**: Integrate interactive features for administrators to delve into data and unearth hidden trends.
3. **Clarity**: Ensure visualizations are lucid, succinct, and easily comprehensible, even for non-technical users.
4. **Performance**: Optimize visualization code to prevent any sluggishness in the admin dashboard.

The infusion of advanced data visualization within the Django admin dashboard is a formidable strategy that transforms data into actionable insights. Whether utilizing libraries like Matplotlib for static charts or Plotly for interactive dashboards, the ability to convey data visually equips administrators with the tools needed to scrutinize, dissect, and make informed choices. By amalgamating robust data management with compelling visualizations, you fortify your mastery in constructing comprehensive web solutions that epitomize excellence on both the backend and frontend fronts.

Securing the admin interface for superusers and staff

Enhancing Admin Interface Security: Safeguarding Superusers and Staff in Django

In the realm of web application development, security remains an unshakable foundation. Robust security measures are paramount to shield confidential data, uphold user privacy, and counter potential threats. Django, recognized for its staunch security focus, empowers developers to erect fortified admin interfaces, ensuring exclusive access to authorized personnel like superusers and staff. This chapter navigates through the intricate strategies and mechanisms employed to bolster admin interface security, cementing the application's integrity and data protection.

Navigating Access Control:

Access control plays a pivotal role in preserving the sanctity of the admin interface. Django's intricate permission system structures user roles, enabling meticulous control over authorized actions and restricted areas. By wielding these permissions, developers can prevent unauthorized entry and allocate varying levels of authority based on roles.

User Roles and Permissions:

Django presents an array of predefined permissions, encompassing add, change, and delete rights for models. These permissions can be assigned at both model and object levels. Custom permissions can also be devised to suit application-specific needs.

Illustration: Crafting Custom Permissions:

python

```python
# models.py
from django.db import models
from django.contrib.auth.models import Permission

class CustomPermission(models.Model):
    name = models.CharField(max_length=100)
    description = models.TextField()

class MyModel(models.Model):
    # Fields and attributes
    class Meta:
        permissions = [
            ("can_view_custom_permission", "Can View Custom Permission"),
        ]
```

In this instance, a bespoke permission named can_view_custom_permission is introduced. This permission can be granted to users holding the corresponding authorization.

Refined Control with @permission_required:

Django's @permission_required decorator furnishes nuanced access control for views. It empowers specification of the requisite permission for view access. Views adorned with this decorator remain off-limits to users lacking the designated permission.

Illustration: Constricting View Access with @permission_required:

python

```python
# views.py
from django.contrib.auth.decorators import permission_required
from django.http import HttpResponse

@permission_required('app_name.can_view_custom_permission')
def restricted_view(request):
    return HttpResponse("Access granted only to users with custom permission.")
```

In this case, the restricted_view is exclusively accessible by users possessing the can_view_custom_permission permission.

Harnessing the @user_passes_test Decorator:

The @user_passes_test decorator confers access control based on a custom function gauging whether a user fulfills specific conditions. This proves invaluable for implementing intricate access rules.

Illustration: Enacting Access Criteria with @user_passes_test:

python

```
# views.py
from django.contrib.auth.decorators import
user_passes_test
from django.http import HttpResponse

def is_staff_user(user):
    return user.is_staff

@user_passes_test(is_staff_user)
def staff_view(request):
    return HttpResponse("Exclusive to staff users.")
```

In this scenario, the staff_view is exclusively accessible to staff users as evaluated by the is_staff_user function.

Securing the admin interface for superusers and staff within Django is a sophisticated yet indispensable endeavor. By tapping into Django's robust permission framework, custom permissions, and access control decorators, administrators can enact stringent security protocols. Limiting entry to authorized personnel safeguards applications from potential breaches and unwarranted actions. Embracing these security mechanisms not only ensures data integrity but also exemplifies dedication to constructing top-tier web solutions that place a premium on user privacy and data safeguarding.

Chapter Three

Building RESTful APIs with DRF
Designing and implementing powerful and flexible APIs

In the contemporary realm of web development, the capacity to craft APIs (Application Programming Interfaces) that are both potent and adaptable stands as a paramount endeavor. APIs act as the conduit that links applications, enabling seamless interactions and data exchange. Django, renowned for its versatility, furnishes developers with the tools to conceptualize APIs that not only facilitate interactions with external entities but also adapt to changing requirements with finesse. This chapter delves into the intricacies of conceptualizing and actualizing APIs within the Django framework, propelling you into a dimension where data flows seamlessly and functionalities remain responsive and malleable.

The Essence of Robust APIs:

A robust API encapsulates the core functionalities of your application, affording external systems the privilege of interacting with it seamlessly. A meticulously designed API abstracts complexities, offering an intuitive and streamlined interface that conceals underlying intricacies.

Selecting API Frameworks:

Within the realm of Django, the Django Rest Framework (DRF) takes center stage as an indispensable toolkit for formulating resilient APIs. DRF expedites the API development journey with its embedded features, encompassing serialization, authentication, and viewsets. The framework facilitates the construction of APIs that align with the principles of REST (Representational State Transfer), ensuring standardized and lucid interactions.

Serialization Unveiled:

Serialization, in the context of Django's API landscape, refers to the process of converting intricate data structures, such as Django models, into formats that are easily consumable, like JSON. DRF's serializers empower you to delineate how data should be presented within API responses.

Illustration: Crafting a Serializer with DRF:

python

```
# serializers.py
from rest_framework import serializers
from .models import Product

class ProductSerializer(serializers.ModelSerializer):
    class Meta:
        model = Product
        fields = '__all__'
```

In this instance, the ProductSerializer transmutes instances of the Product model into JSON renditions.

API Construction with Viewsets:

DRF's viewsets streamline the process of API formulation by amalgamating common actions like listing, creation, update, and deletion into a singular class. Viewsets not only simplify the API structure but also foster concise and efficient coding practices.

Illustration: Crafting a Viewset with DRF:

python

```python
# views.py
from rest_framework import viewsets
from .models import Product
from .serializers import ProductSerializer

class ProductViewSet(viewsets.ModelViewSet):
    queryset = Product.objects.all()
    serializer_class = ProductSerializer
```

In this example, the ProductViewSet amalgamates diverse operations pertinent to the Product model.

Authentication and Permissions:

A pivotal facet of API design entails authentication and permissions. DRF offers an array of authentication mechanisms, including token-based authentication and OAuth. Permissions serve as the gatekeepers that ensure only authorized users gain access to designated endpoints.

Illustration: Implementing Token Authentication:

python

```
# settings.py
REST_FRAMEWORK = {
    'DEFAULT_AUTHENTICATION_CLASSES': [

'rest_framework.authentication.TokenAuthentication',
    ],
}
```

By incorporating the TokenAuthentication class into the roster of authentication classes, token-based authentication is instituted.

Versioning and Documentation:

A robust API is one that evolves organically. DRF supports versioning, enabling you to implement modifications without disrupting existing clients. Additionally, DRF provides tools to facilitate automatic API documentation generation through mechanisms like DRF's inbuilt BrowsableAPIRenderer or third-party solutions like Swagger.

The process of designing and realizing potent and adaptable APIs within Django ushers in an era of seamless integration, data harmonization, and application interactions. By harnessing resources like the Django Rest Framework, you can fashion APIs that not only comply with REST principles but also underscore scalability, versioning, and meticulous documentation. With serialization, viewsets, authentication, and permissions at your disposal, you are poised to shape APIs that empower your application to communicate seamlessly with external ecosystems. Constructing APIs that encapsulate your application's core functionalities while perpetuating dynamism and versatility is a testament to your expertise in crafting high-caliber web solutions that excel within the interconnected digital domain.

Versioning and documentation of your APIs for external use

In the landscape of contemporary web development, the evolution of APIs (Application Programming Interfaces) assumes a dynamic character. As applications expand and evolve, sustaining compatibility with existing clients emerges as a pivotal priority. Within the realm of Django, renowned for its precision and adaptability, developers are endowed with the means to handle API versioning seamlessly and deliver comprehensive documentation for external consumption. This chapter delves into the intricate realm of versioning and documentation within the Django API domain, fostering harmonious interactions and cultivating user-friendly experiences for developers and end-users alike.

Strategies for Seamless Evolution: API Versioning

API versioning constitutes a strategic maneuver to navigate the terrain of changes within your API while upholding the continuity for established clients. It facilitates the introduction of enhancements and modifications without causing disruptions in the functionality of prior versions.

Distinct Approaches to API Versioning

- URL-based Versioning: This approach entails indicating the version within the API endpoint URL. For instance, api/v1/endpoint/ signifies version 1, while api/v2/endpoint/ signifies version 2.
- Header-based Versioning: The version is communicated through an HTTP header, such as Accept or X-API-Version.
- Media Type Versioning: Diverse media types (MIME types) are employed to differentiate between versions.

Exemplifying URL-based Versioning

python

```python
# urls.py
from django.urls import path
from . import views

urlpatterns = [
    path('api/v1/endpoint/',
views.EndpointV1.as_view(), name='v1_endpoint'),
    path('api/v2/endpoint/',
views.EndpointV2.as_view(), name='v2_endpoint'),
]
```

In this instance, two versions of the endpoint API are provided through the mechanism of URL-based versioning.

Unveiling Comprehensive Documentation: The Key to Clarity

Comprehensive documentation serves as the backbone of seamless API integration. Well-crafted documentation equips developers to comprehend endpoints, payloads, authentication protocols, and response structures.

Harnessing the Power of DRF's BrowsableAPIRenderer

The Django Rest Framework (DRF) introduces the BrowsableAPIRenderer, a tool that generates interactive API documentation. This renderer furnishes a web-based interface for exploring APIs, testing endpoints, and grasping the intricacies of request and response frameworks.

Example: Integrating BrowsableAPIRenderer

python

```
# settings.py
REST_FRAMEWORK = {
    'DEFAULT_RENDERER_CLASSES': [
        'rest_framework.renderers.JSONRenderer',

'rest_framework.renderers.BrowsableAPIRenderer',
    ],
}
```

By including BrowsableAPIRenderer within the list of DEFAULT_RENDERER_CLASSES, the API documentation becomes accessible via the browser.

Leveraging Third-Party Documentation Aids

While the BrowsableAPIRenderer presents substantial value, third-party tools like Swagger (OpenAPI) and Postman provide enriched functionalities. Swagger facilitates automatic documentation generation alongside an interactive UI, while Postman streamlines API testing and documentation collaboration.

Example: Integrating Swagger for API Documentation

python

```python
# settings.py
INSTALLED_APPS = [
    # ...
    'drf_yasg',
]

# urls.py
from django.urls import path
from . import views
from rest_framework import permissions
from drf_yasg.views import get_schema_view
from drf_yasg import openapi

schema_view = get_schema_view(
    openapi.Info(
        title="Your API",
        default_version='v1',
        description="Your API description",
```

```
terms_of_service="https://www.yourapp.com/terms/",
contact=openapi.Contact(email="contact@yourapp.com"),
        license=openapi.License(name="Your License"),
    ),
    public=True,
    permission_classes=(permissions.AllowAny,),
)

urlpatterns = [
    path('swagger/', schema_view.with_ui('swagger',
cache_timeout=0), name='schema-swagger-ui'),
    # ...
]
```

By integrating the drf_yasg package, you can seamlessly generate Swagger documentation for your API.

Effectively handling API versioning and crafting meticulous documentation within the Django realm stand as pivotal elements in fabricating robust, adaptable, and user-friendly APIs. Versioning empowers the evolutionary journey of APIs sans disruption to existing clients, while thorough documentation equips developers to seamlessly weave APIs into their applications. Harnessing tools such as DRF's BrowsableAPIRenderer, Swagger, and Postman elevates the documentation experience by furnishing interactive platforms for exploring APIs and testing endpoints. Embracing these practices during your API development odyssey signifies your dedication to delivering APIs that embody not only potency and flexibility but also intuitive clarity for external users and developers alike.

Securing and throttling API endpoints for production use

In the contemporary landscape of web development, the safeguarding of API (Application Programming Interface) endpoints holds significant prominence. Ensuring the security and controlled usage of these endpoints is instrumental in maintaining data integrity and application stability within production environments. Django, renowned for its robust capabilities and emphasis on security, offers a comprehensive set of tools for fortifying and overseeing API endpoints with precision. In this chapter, we delve into the nuanced facets of ensuring security and managing usage through throttling in Django's framework. This process erects a protective bastion suitable for production contexts, upholding seamless interactions while maintaining an elevated level of security.

The Core Tenet of API Security:

API security forms the bedrock of sustaining data confidentiality, integrity, and availability during the exchange between applications. Warding off unauthorized access, data breaches, and malicious intrusions is pivotal in safeguarding the trustworthiness and reliability of an application.

Enforcing Authentication:

Django's authentication framework is equipped with a spectrum of authentication methods aimed at verifying the identity of clients accessing API endpoints. These methods encompass token-based authentication, session-based authentication, and OAuth2.

Illustrative Token-Based Authentication Scenario:

python

```python
# settings.py
REST_FRAMEWORK = {
    'DEFAULT_AUTHENTICATION_CLASSES': [

'rest_framework.authentication.TokenAuthentication',
    ],
}
```

By integrating TokenAuthentication into the roster of authentication classes, the door is opened to token-based authentication.

Authorization and Access Control:

While authentication validates identity, authorization governs the extent of access. Django's permissions framework empowers the definition of granular access controls for varying user roles.

Example: Custom Permissions for API Endpoints

python

```python
# views.py
from rest_framework import permissions

class YourApiView(APIView):
    permission_classes =
```

```
[permissions.IsAuthenticatedOrReadOnly]
```

In this instance, the IsAuthenticatedOrReadOnly permission grants read-only access to unauthenticated users and full access to authenticated users.

Strategic Throttling for Controlled Interaction:

API throttling entails the regulation of the rate at which clients can make requests to an API. This mechanism serves as a deterrent against misuse and excessive resource utilization, ensuring an equitable distribution of resources.

Incorporating Throttling Example:

python

```python
# settings.py
REST_FRAMEWORK = {
    'DEFAULT_THROTTLE_CLASSES': [
        'rest_framework.throttling.UserRateThrottle',
        'rest_framework.throttling.AnonRateThrottle',
    ],
    'DEFAULT_THROTTLE_RATES': {
        'user': '1000/day',
        'anon': '100/day',
    },
}
```

In this configuration, UserRateThrottle confines authenticated users to 1000 requests per day, while AnonRateThrottle restricts unauthenticated users to 100 requests daily.

Shielding from CORS Intrusion:

Cross-Origin Resource Sharing (CORS) acts as a security measure to prevent unsanctioned access to server resources from external domains. The django-cors-headers package within Django aids in configuring CORS settings to mitigate cross-domain requests.

Exemplary CORS Protection Configuration:

python

```python
# settings.py
INSTALLED_APPS = [
    # ...
    'corsheaders',
]

MIDDLEWARE = [
    # ...
    'corsheaders.middleware.CorsMiddleware',
    # ...
]

CORS_ALLOWED_ORIGINS = [
    "https://yourdomain.com",
]
```

In this setup, the CORS middleware is integrated to regulate the domains that can access the API.

Rate Limiting: Balancing Act for Optimization:

Throttling emerges as a strategic solution to manage request rates, assuring consistent performance and preventing abrupt spikes in traffic.

The process of enhancing and controlling API endpoints within the Django framework encompasses a tactical approach to securing against unauthorized access, malicious intent, and resource overconsumption. By instituting authentication, authorization, and throttling strategies, a fortified environment is created for API endpoints, fostering user confidence and reliability. Through the utilization of Django's inherent security features and the application of tools like CORS protection and rate limiting, a fortress of protection is erected against potential vulnerabilities. This array of practices showcases your dedication to formulating top-tier web solutions adept at thriving within production contexts, promoting secure and seamless data interchange while preserving the robustness of the application.

Chapter Four

Asynchronous Programming in Django
Understanding asynchronous programming and Django's async features

In the ever-evolving landscape of contemporary web development, the significance of asynchronous programming has soared as applications aspire to offer impeccable user experiences. Asynchronous programming, renowned for its capacity to execute multiple tasks concurrently without causing blockages in execution, has become a cornerstone for constructing high-performance web applications. Within this chapter, we embark on a journey to fathom the intricacies of asynchronous programming, unveil the asynchronous capabilities embedded in Django, and delve into the manner in which these attributes amplify the efficacy and responsiveness of web applications.

Decoding the Essence of Asynchronous Programming:

The conventional paradigm of synchronous programming involves the sequential execution of tasks. However, the advent of asynchronous programming has ushered in a new era, allowing tasks to run concurrently, thereby enhancing overall application efficiency, especially when tasks are time-intensive or reliant on external resources.

Harvesting the Benefits of Asynchronous Programming:

1. **Parallelism**: Asynchronous programming facilitates parallel execution, optimizing resource utilization.
2. **I/O-Intensive Tasks**: Asynchronous operations are particularly advantageous for I/O-intensive tasks such as database queries and API calls.
3. **Non-Blocking Nature**: Asynchronous tasks operate without impeding the execution of other tasks, thereby heightening responsiveness.

Delving into the Asynchronous Realms of Django:

Django, renowned for its synchronous nature, embraced the realm of asynchronicity with the advent of version 3.1. This ushered in a new era where asynchronous views, database queries, and template rendering play pivotal roles.

Asynchronous Views:

python

```
# views.py
from django.http import JsonResponse
from asgiref.sync import async_to_sync
import asyncio

async def async_view(request):
    await asyncio.sleep(2)
    return JsonResponse({'message': 'Asynchronous View Concluded'})

sync_view = async_to_sync(async_view)
```

In this illustrative example, the async_view incorporates asynchronous await for a sleep operation, simulating an asynchronous task. Employing the async_to_sync decorator converts the asynchronous view into a synchronous one, facilitating harmonious coexistence within Django's synchronous context.

Asynchronous Database Queries:

python

```
# views.py
from django.db import connection

async def async_db_query(request):
    async with connection.cursor() as cursor:
        await cursor.execute('SELECT * FROM my_table')
        results = await cursor.fetchall()
    return JsonResponse({'results': results})
```

This segment elucidates the art of asynchronous database queries through the utilization of the async with context manager. This empowers the execution of asynchronous queries sans obstruction of concurrent tasks.

Asynchronous Template Rendering:

python

```
# views.py
from django.template import loader
from django.http import HttpResponse

async def async_template(request):
```

```
    template = loader.get_template('my_template.html')
    context = {'variable': 'Asynchronous Template
Rendering'}
    rendered_template = await
template.render_async(context)
    return HttpResponse(rendered_template)
```

In this context, the asynchronous rendering of templates is masterfully orchestrated via the render_async method.

Choosing the Right Path for Asynchronous Endeavors in Django:

The integration of asynchronous programming into Django thrives when dealing with tasks demanding interaction with external resources, such as database queries, API invocations, or file operations. However, the universal application of asynchronous implementation is not mandatory. Asynchronous programming merits consideration when:

1. **Concurrent Operations Prove Fruitful**: The application's performance stands to gain from the concurrent execution of tasks.
2. **I/O Operations Prevail**: Asynchronous methodologies prove invaluable for tasks rooted in I/O operations that would otherwise halt the main thread.
3. **Scalability Takes Center Stage**: Asynchronous code can usher in remarkable scalability enhancements, facilitating the handling of elevated request volumes.

Navigating the Complex Terrain and Upholding Prudent Measures:

Asynchronous programming brings an array of advantages, yet concurrently introduces complexities, including the orchestration of asynchronous code flow and the preservation of thread safety. Furthermore, certain libraries and packages may not seamlessly align with asynchronous contexts, necessitating thoughtful deliberation before initiation.

In the Final Analysis:

Asynchronous programming has solidified its stature as a pivotal paradigm in contemporary web development, championing efficiency, responsiveness, and scalability. Django's integration of asynchronous attributes stands as a testament to its evolutionary trajectory in constructing high-performance applications. A comprehensive grasp of asynchronous views, database queries, and template rendering empowers developers to harness Django's full asynchronous potential. By adroitly selecting scenarios primed for asynchronous adoption and skillfully managing the intricacies of asynchronous code, developers can birth web solutions that embody both velocity and sophistication, underscoring Django's transformation into an adaptable and dynamic web framework.

Building asynchronous views, tasks, and WebSocket handling

In the ever-evolving sphere of modern web development, the pursuit of responsive and high-efficiency applications remains paramount. Within this context emerges the concept of asynchronous programming, a dynamic approach that redefines how web applications tackle simultaneous tasks and real-time interactions. This chapter delves into the intricate realm of crafting asynchronous views, tasks, and WebSocket management within the confines of the Django framework. By emphasizing efficiency, scalability, and real-time responsiveness, developers will uncover the prowess of these asynchronous elements, thereby propelling the user experience to unprecedented heights.

Unraveling the Enigma of Asynchronous Views:

Amid the tapestry of web development, asynchronous views stand as a beacon of agility and performance. Traditional synchronous views tread the path of sequential task execution, often leading to bottlenecks and diminished responsiveness during resource-intensive tasks. In stark contrast, asynchronous views usher in a new era by empowering tasks to unfurl concurrently without impeding the primary thread of application execution. The upshot? Substantial enhancement in application responsiveness and overall user experience.

A Glimpse of Asynchronous Views in Action:

python

```python
# views.py
from django.http import JsonResponse
import asyncio

async def async_view(request):
    await asyncio.sleep(2)
    return JsonResponse({'message': 'Asynchronous View Completed'})
```

In this illustrative instance, the async_view employs the await mechanism to simulate an asynchronous task encompassing a 2-second sleep operation. This pivotal step ensures that the application remains responsive while the time-intensive task is diligently carried out.

Harnessing the Dynamic Realm of Asynchronous Tasks:

Enter asynchronous tasks, a cornerstone of building high-performance web applications. By delegating resource-intensive tasks to the background, the primary thread remains unburdened, paving the way for a seamlessly fluid user experience. These tasks find their niche in activities such as email dispatch, data processing, and resource-heavy computations.

Breathing Life into Asynchronous Task Dynamics:

python

```python
# tasks.py
from celery import shared_task
import time

@shared_task
def asynchronous_task():
    time.sleep(5)
    return 'Asynchronous Task Completed'
```

In this narrative, the asynchronous_task collaborates harmoniously with the Celery library to extricate the time-consuming operation from the application's main context. The result? An application that remains agile and responsive, even during resource-intensive tasks.

Navigating the Waters of Real-Time Engagement: WebSocket Management:

WebSocket handling unfurls a portal to real-time communication between clients and servers. Distinct from the traditional landscape of HTTP requests, WebSocket connections stand resiliently ajar, offering a conduit for seamless and two-way data exchange. This transformative capability equips applications with the tools required for real-time updates—chat applications, live notifications, and collaborative platforms being prime exemplars.

Diving into Django's WebSocket Management:

python

```python
# consumers.py
from channels.generic.websocket import
AsyncWebsocketConsumer

class ChatConsumer(AsyncWebsocketConsumer):
    async def connect(self):
        await self.accept()

    async def disconnect(self, close_code):
        pass

    async def receive(self, text_data):
        await self.send(text_data='You said: ' +
text_data)
```

In this vibrant tableau, the ChatConsumer takes center stage, offering a blueprint for constructing WebSocket consumers. The connect method ushers in the WebSocket connection, while the receive method assumes responsibility for responding to incoming data by promptly echoing it back to the client.

Embracing the Lustrous Symphony of Asynchrony:

Crafting asynchronous views, tasks, and WebSocket management encapsulates the essence of efficient and responsive web application development. Asynchronous views extend a responsive veneer to the application even during resource-intensive tasks. Asynchronous tasks confer a performance boost by rerouting time-intensive duties to dedicated workers, thereby sustaining user interaction fluidity. Simultaneously, WebSocket management elevates applications to the echelons of real-time communication, surmounting the barriers posed by traditional request-response paradigms.

Navigating Challenges and Espousing Best Practices:

While the manifold benefits of asynchronous components are evident, mastering them demands a delicate dance with complexities, including the orchestration of asynchronous code sequences and the vigilant preservation of thread safety. The judicious selection of scenarios primed for asynchronous intervention is crucial for optimal performance without undue complication.

Asynchronous views, tasks, and WebSocket management stand as the pillars bolstering efficiency and interactivity in contemporary web development. By adroitly incorporating these components into the Django framework, developers forge an environment conducive to applications that respond briskly, navigate resource-intensive tasks seamlessly, and foster real-time interactions. As the clarion call for high-performance applications continues to resonate, the embrace of the asynchronous paradigm isn't merely strategic—it's an imperative step in architecting web solutions that exude both swiftness and sophistication.

Deploying and scaling asynchronous applications

In the dynamic world of web development, the orchestration of asynchronous applications stands as a cornerstone for bolstering performance and scalability. The symbiotic relationship between asynchronous programming and application deployment heralds a new era of responsiveness and efficiency. In this chapter, we embark on a voyage through the intricacies of deploying and scaling asynchronous applications within the Django framework. By delving into strategies for deployment, techniques for scaling, and methods for optimizing performance, we delve into the art of proficiently harnessing the capabilities of asynchronicity.

Strategizing for Deployment:

Effective deployment of asynchronous applications necessitates careful consideration of the underlying infrastructure. The choice of a deployment platform that supports the nuances of asynchronous programming is crucial for creating a seamless execution environment.

Diverse Deployment Platforms and Their Implications:

python

```
# Dockerfile
# Select a foundational image compatible with
asynchronous applications
FROM python:3.9

# Set the working directory
WORKDIR /app

# Install essential dependencies
COPY requirements.txt .
RUN pip install -r requirements.txt

# Integrate the application code
COPY . .

# Specify the command to execute the application
CMD ["uvicorn", "app.main:app", "--host", "0.0.0.0", "-
-port", "8000"]
```

This illustrative example showcases an asynchronous application's deployment using the UVicorn ASGI server. The Dockerfile outlines the image's construction and defines the command for running the application.

Scaling for Agility and Responsiveness:

Efficiently scaling asynchronous applications enhances their performance and agility, ensuring optimal resource utilization even during surges in user activity. Employing strategies like load balancing, auto-scaling, and distributed architectures plays a pivotal role in maintaining a seamless application experience.

Load Balancing Magic with NGINX:

nginx

```
# nginx.conf
upstream backend {
  server backend1.example.com;
  server backend2.example.com;
}

server {
  listen 80;
  location / {
    proxy_pass http://backend;
  }
}
```

The utilization of NGINX for load balancing evenly distributes incoming requests across multiple instances, thereby enhancing overall performance.

Leveraging Celery for Efficient Task Execution:

python

```
# tasks.py
from celery import Celery

app = Celery('tasks',
broker='pyamqp://guest@localhost//')
```

```
@app.task
def asynchronous_task():
    # Task execution logic here
```

Celery, a well-regarded distributed task queue, facilitates the scaling of asynchronous tasks. By distributing tasks among multiple workers, applications can deftly manage heightened workloads.

Fine-Tuning for Optimal Performance:

Optimization is the crux of bolstering the efficiency of asynchronous applications. To this end, profiling, caching, and the adept utilization of appropriate asynchronous libraries all play a role in enhancing performance.

Unveiling Insights through Profiling and Monitoring:

Leveraging tools like the Django Debug Toolbar or performance monitoring platforms aids developers in pinpointing performance bottlenecks and optimizing resource consumption.

Caching for Heightened Responsiveness:

python

```
# views.py
from django.core.cache import cache
```

```
def cached_view(request):
    cached_data = cache.get('cached_data')
    if not cached_data:
        cached_data = expensive_calculation()
        cache.set('cached_data', cached_data,
timeout=3600)
    return JsonResponse({'data': cached_data})
```

By employing caching mechanisms, such as those provided by Django's caching framework, applications can minimize redundant computations, leading to a more responsive experience.

Choosing Prudently Among Asynchronous Libraries:

Optimal selection of asynchronous libraries significantly impacts an application's performance. Libraries like asyncio and uvloop amplify asynchronous code execution, elevating speed and efficiency.

The deployment and scaling of asynchronous applications mark a pivotal phase in fully harnessing the power of asynchronous programming. By astutely selecting deployment platforms, implementing sound scaling strategies, and fine-tuning performance, developers elevate user experiences, ensuring that applications remain responsive and efficient even during periods of high demand. Masterfully orchestrated asynchronous applications not only meet the expectations of modern web users but also thrive in an environment where agility, efficiency, and seamless scalability are paramount.

Chapter Five

Real-Time Features with Channels
Implementing real-time features using Django Channels

In the ever-evolving arena of web applications, the call for real-time engagement has given rise to an era of heightened interactivity and user immersion. Django Channels, an extension of the Django framework, emerges as a valuable tool for infusing real-time capabilities into applications. In this chapter, we embark on a journey to comprehend the implementation of real-time features using Django Channels, exploring its architecture, WebSocket handling, and its seamless integration with Celery for efficient background task processing. By becoming proficient in these aspects, developers can construct applications that offer seamless, responsive, and captivating real-time interactions.

Delving into Django Channels:

Conventional Django applications adhere to synchronous request-response patterns, which can impose limitations when striving to incorporate real-time features. Enter Django Channels, which introduces an asynchronous layer to manage multiple connections concurrently. This empowers developers to craft applications capable of delivering dynamic and interactive experiences through real-time updates.

The Blueprint of Django Channels' Architecture:

Django Channels introduces a crucial concept – consumers. These asynchronous functions are tasked with handling incoming messages and orchestrating diverse actions. Through routing, messages of varying types are directed to their corresponding consumers, ensuring streamlined communication.

Navigating WebSocket Management with Django Channels:

WebSocket, the protocol facilitating bidirectional data exchange, forms the backbone of real-time features. The wings of Django Channels unfurl through the ChannelsWebSocketConsumer, a mechanism that simplifies the management of WebSocket connections.

python

```python
# consumers.py
from channels.generic.websocket import
AsyncWebsocketConsumer

class RealTimeConsumer(AsyncWebsocketConsumer):
    async def connect(self):
        await self.accept()

    async def disconnect(self, close_code):
        pass

    async def receive(self, text_data):
```

```
await self.send(text_data=text_data)
```

In this instance, the RealTimeConsumer class, acting as a rudimentary WebSocket consumer, echoes received messages back to the client.

A Fusion of Django Channels and Celery:

The beauty of Django Channels lies in its seamless compatibility with Celery – a distributed task queue. This alliance permits the delegation of resource-intensive tasks to background workers, ensuring that real-time interactions retain their responsiveness.

python

```python
# consumers.py
from channels.generic.websocket import
AsyncWebsocketConsumer
from myapp.tasks import heavy_processing_task

class RealTimeConsumer(AsyncWebsocketConsumer):
    async def connect(self):
        await self.accept()

    async def receive(self, text_data):
        await self.send(text_data="Task initiated.
Check back shortly.")
        await heavy_processing_task.delay(text_data)
        await self.send(text_data="Task completed.
Results ready.")
```

In this revised example, the heavy_processing_task is dispatched to a Celery worker, enabling the WebSocket connection to remain responsive.

Casting a Broadcast Spell for Real-Time Updates:

Django Channels elevates the game by allowing the broadcasting of real-time updates to multiple clients concurrently. Through the establishment of a channel layer, messages can be disseminated to specific channels, subsequently accessed by subscribing clients.

python

```python
# consumers.py
from channels.generic.websocket import
AsyncWebsocketConsumer

class RealTimeConsumer(AsyncWebsocketConsumer):
    async def connect(self):
        self.room_name =
self.scope['url_route']['kwargs']['room_name']
        self.room_group_name = f"chat_{self.room_name}"

        await self.channel_layer.group_add(
            self.room_group_name,
            self.channel_name
        )

        await self.accept()

    async def disconnect(self, close_code):
        await self.channel_layer.group_discard(
            self.room_group_name,
            self.channel_name
        )

    async def receive(self, text_data):
        await self.channel_layer.group_send(
            self.room_group_name,
            {
                'type': 'chat_message',
                'message': text_data
```

```
          }
       )

  async def chat_message(self, event):
      message = event['message']

      await self.send(text_data=message)
```

In this extended rendition, the RealTimeConsumer not only manages individual client interactions but also disseminates messages to all clients subscribed to the same channel group.

Elevating Experiences through Real-Time Features:

With Django Channels as the conduit, the creation of real-time features propels applications toward delivering dynamic and interactive user experiences. By embracing Django Channels' asynchronous essence, developers forge applications capable of seamless communication of updates, fostering real-time interactions, and maintaining unswerving responsiveness even during strenuous workloads. Through the synergy of Django Channels and Celery, application efficiency is fortified, enabling the offloading of resource-intensive tasks to the background, while preserving real-time reactivity. The mastery of Django Channels empowers developers to unearth the potential of crafting applications that shine bright within the contemporary landscape of web development.

Building chat applications and handling WebSocket connections

In the realm of dynamic web applications, the call for real-time communication has surged, igniting the emergence of engaging and interactive chat platforms. Django Channels, an extension of the Django framework, emerges as a potent tool for shaping such applications by facilitating the seamless management of WebSocket connections. This chapter embarks on an exploration of constructing chat applications using Django Channels, unraveling the architecture of real-time messaging, orchestrating the synchronization of diverse clients, and unveiling strategies for ensuring a fluid exchange of information. By mastering the art of building chat applications and deftly navigating WebSocket connections, developers can engineer immersive, responsive, and captivating user experiences.

Designing Architectures for Real-Time Chat Platforms:

Central to the allure of real-time chat applications is the ability to exchange messages instantaneously between users. The asynchronous nature of Django Channels and its adept handling of WebSocket connections lay the foundation for this fluid communication.

WebSocket Handling Redefined with Django Channels:

WebSocket, the protocol that facilitates bidirectional communication, serves as the backbone of real-time chat applications. Django Channels streamlines WebSocket management through the use of consumers, which are responsible for processing incoming messages and orchestrating the requisite actions.

python

```python
# consumers.py
from channels.generic.websocket import
AsyncWebsocketConsumer

class ChatConsumer(AsyncWebsocketConsumer):
    async def connect(self):
        await self.accept()

    async def disconnect(self, close_code):
        pass

    async def receive(self, text_data):
        await self.send(text_data=text_data)
```

In this foundational example, the ChatConsumer class encapsulates the essentials of WebSocket handling. Upon establishing a connection, it acknowledges incoming WebSocket connections and echoes received messages back to the originating source.

Crafting Harmonized Chat Environments:

The charm of chat applications lies in the capacity to engage multiple users within a shared chat room, fostering synchronized interactions. Django Channels empowers this synchrony by introducing the notion of groups, facilitating the management and synchronization of messages across users.

python

```python
# consumers.py
from channels.generic.websocket import
AsyncWebsocketConsumer
```

```python
class ChatConsumer(AsyncWebsocketConsumer):
    async def connect(self):
        self.room_name =
self.scope['url_route']['kwargs']['room_name']
        self.room_group_name = f"chat_{self.room_name}"

        await self.channel_layer.group_add(
            self.room_group_name,
            self.channel_name
        )

        await self.accept()

    async def disconnect(self, close_code):
        await self.channel_layer.group_discard(
            self.room_group_name,
            self.channel_name
        )

    async def receive(self, text_data):
        await self.channel_layer.group_send(
            self.room_group_name,
            {
                'type': 'chat_message',
                'message': text_data
            }
        )

    async def chat_message(self, event):
        message = event['message']

        await self.send(text_data=message)
```

In this extended illustration, the ChatConsumer not only steers individual client interactions but also disseminates messages to all participants within the shared chat room.

Integrating User Authentication and Ensuring Security:

Secure interactions often entail user authentication for maintaining the integrity of the platform. Django Channels facilitates the authentication of WebSocket connections and the responsible handling of user-specific data within the consumers.

python

```python
# consumers.py
from channels.generic.websocket import
AsyncWebsocketConsumer

class ChatConsumer(AsyncWebsocketConsumer):
    async def connect(self):
        if self.scope['user'].is_anonymous:
            await self.close()
        else:
            await self.accept()
```

In this script excerpt, the connect method undertakes user authentication verification before granting WebSocket connection approval.

The craft of constructing chat applications and adeptly navigating WebSocket connections opens doors to dynamic and interactive real-time exchanges. Leveraging Django Channels' asynchronous capabilities and its proficient WebSocket management, developers can sculpt applications that foster seamless interaction among users. The harmonization of chat rooms, user authentication, and secure message transmission collectively contribute to the creation of captivating and secure chat experiences. By mastering the art of WebSocket connections, developers endow their applications with the prowess to facilitate real-time conversations, fostering engagement and user satisfaction within the ever-evolving sphere of contemporary web development.

Integrating Channels with Celery for background task processing

In the swiftly evolving arena of web development, the pursuit of applications that effortlessly blend real-time capabilities with effective background task management has become a pivotal endeavor. Within this context, Django Channels and Celery emerge as a dynamic duo, bestowing developers with the ability to craft applications that not only deliver real-time interactions but also gracefully handle resource-intensive tasks in the background. This chapter embarks on an exploration of the intricacies surrounding the integration of Django Channels and Celery, unveiling the architectural intricacies of this partnership, executing background tasks, and unleashing the potential of applications that exhibit responsiveness and high-performance attributes.

The Harmony of Channels and Celery:

Django Channels, conceived to introduce asynchronous capabilities to Django applications, enriches the digital landscape with real-time functionalities. Conversely, Celery presents itself as a robust distributed task queue, excelling in the art of asynchronous task processing. The marriage of these two technological facets engenders a formidable platform that adeptly juggles real-time interactions and background tasks with an air of seamlessness.

Background Task Execution with Celery:

Celery's forte shines through when tasked with unburdening the primary application thread from resource-intensive obligations. Be it dispatching emails, generating intricate reports, or executing elaborate computations, Celery orchestrates these tasks with finesse, ensuring their execution without compromising the responsiveness of the application.

python

```python
# tasks.py
from celery import shared_task

@shared_task
def process_data(data):
    # ... execute data processing ...
    return result
```

In this instance, the process_data function is earmarked as a shared task, signifying its capability to be carried out asynchronously by Celery workers.

Enriching Channels with Celery:

The harmonious integration of Celery with Django Channels bestows the application with the prowess to offload time-consuming tasks from WebSocket consumers. This ensures that WebSocket connections remain agile and responsive, even amidst surges in demand.

python

```
# consumers.py
from channels.generic.websocket import
AsyncWebsocketConsumer
from myapp.tasks import process_data

class RealTimeConsumer(AsyncWebsocketConsumer):
    async def connect(self):
        await self.accept()

    async def receive(self, text_data):
        await self.send(text_data="Task initiation in
progress. Check back shortly.")
        result = await process_data.delay(text_data)
        await self.send(text_data=f"Task accomplished.
Outcome: {result}")
```

In this scenario, the process_data task is delegated to a Celery worker through the employment of the delay method. This orchestrates a scenario wherein the WebSocket connection remains alert and responsive while the background task gracefully unfolds.

Ensuring Fluid Synchronization:

The amalgamation of Celery and Django Channels gains particular significance when tasked with managing processes that could potentially hinder the core application thread. By delegating these processes to Celery workers, the application remains agile, providing users with an uninterrupted experience.

Error Handling and Oversight:

Celery enters the fray with built-in mechanisms for managing errors and overseeing tasks. Failed tasks can be revisited for another attempt, and the availability of robust monitoring tools furnishes insights into the execution of tasks and the overall health of the system.

The seamless integration of Django Channels and Celery heralds a new chapter in the narrative of web application development. Through the amalgamation of Django Channels' real-time capabilities with Celery's finesse in background task processing, developers are empowered to forge applications that seamlessly oscillate between dynamic, interactive engagements and resource-efficient background task execution. Whether the goal is the creation of chat applications that remain updated in real-time or the delegation of resource-intensive tasks for optimal efficiency, the alliance of Channels and Celery catapults applications toward a realm characterized by enhanced efficiency and user gratification. Armed with the expertise of this fusion, developers position themselves to create applications that impeccably intertwine real-time interactivity with background efficiency, thereby steering the trajectory of web development toward unprecedented frontiers.

Chapter Six

Extending Authentication and Authorization

Implementing Single Sign-On (SSO) and third-party authentication

In the dynamic landscape of contemporary web applications, user authentication takes center stage, shaping security, user interaction, and seamless access to diverse services. As applications burgeon in complexity, the call for smooth authentication mechanisms becomes resounding. Single Sign-On (SSO) and third-party authentication emerge as potent solutions that not only elevate user convenience but also simplify authentication procedures for developers. This chapter embarks on an odyssey to unravel the intricacies of embedding SSO and third-party authentication within the Django framework, plunging into technical nuances while illustrating their pragmatic embodiment.

The Universe of Single Sign-On (SSO):

Single Sign-On embodies a paradigm shift in authentication's realm. It empowers users with access to multiple applications through a solitary set of credentials, obviating the need to juggle myriad usernames and passwords. This process orbits around a central authentication server that bestows entry across diverse applications, streamlining the user experience's cosmic trajectory.

Embedding SSO in Django's Fabric:

For SSO's orchestration, authentication protocols like OAuth2 or OpenID Connect usually grace the stage. Django's ecosystem is enriched with libraries and tools for harmonizing these protocols seamlessly.

python

```python
# settings.py
INSTALLED_APPS = [
    # ...
    'social_django',
]

AUTHENTICATION_BACKENDS = (
    'social_core.backends.open_id.OpenIdAuth',
    'social_core.backends.google.GoogleOAuth2',
    # ...
)
```

Here, the social_django constellation is added to our project's cosmos, while authentication backends for OpenID and Google OAuth2 are invoked, enabling the interstellar communion with OpenID and Google accounts.

Third-Party Authentication's Constellations:

Third-party authentication harnesses the prowess of eminent platforms like Google, Facebook, or Twitter to facilitate user ingress into applications. By furnishing users with the ability to log in through their existing credentials from these celestial bodies, developers hasten user onboarding and augment application adoption.

Integrating Celestial Elements of Third-Party Authentication:

Django's foray into third-party authentication is charioted by libraries like django-allauth and python-social-auth. These libraries usher in comprehensive attributes for seamlessly intertwining third-party gateways into the login milieu.

python

```
# settings.py
INSTALLED_APPS = [
    # ...
    'allauth',
    'allauth.account',
    'allauth.socialaccount',
    'allauth.socialaccount.providers.google',
    # ...
]

AUTHENTICATION_BACKENDS = (
    # ...
'allauth.account.auth_backends.AuthenticationBackend',
    # ...
)
```

In this stellar exhibition, the django-allauth constellation is integrated into the project. Specific providences like Google are interwoven to permit users to authenticate through their astral Google accounts.

Crafting Cosmic User Experience:

Both SSO and third-party authentication don the cloak of customization to align with the application's astral aesthetics and user expectations. This encompasses the tailoring of the login trajectory, the administration of user data, and the steering of data-sharing consent.

Augmenting Security and Compliance's Gravity:

Amidst the convenience gifted by SSO and third-party authentication looms the specter of security concerns. Prudent management of access tokens, refresh tokens, and safeguarding the sanctity of communication between the application and the authentication custodian are paramount. Furthermore, adhering to data protection regulations like GDPR becomes a sine qua non while navigating user data realms.

Stellar Application:

Imagine an interstellar e-commerce haven where users soar into their accounts using their Google celestial passports. Third-party authentication propels users into the galaxy of seamless login, exempting them from birthing new access codes. This unfurls a cosmic welcome mat for new users, kindling user enthusiasm, and fostering a user experience marked by cosmic grandeur.

Infusing Single Sign-On (SSO) and third-party authentication into Django's tapestry empowers developers to sculpt applications that render user access fluid while simplifying authentication metamorphoses. By orchestrating protocols like OAuth2 and leveraging well-recognized realms for authentication, developers expedite user onboarding, amplify security protocols, and orchestrate an experience more akin to stardust. Through meticulous customization and observance of security and privacy constellations, SSO and third-party authentication transmute into powerful quasars in the cosmos of modern web application development. With mastery over these authentication beacons, developers assume the mantle to weave applications that honor user convenience and fortify security, propelling the digital voyage to heights unparalleled.

Customizing user permissions and group-based access control

In the intricate realm of web application development, the intricate art of access control takes center stage. As applications expand in complexity, catering to diverse user roles becomes pivotal. This necessitates a fine-tuned approach to user permissions and access levels, and Django, a robust web framework, equips developers with an array of tools to sculpt access control with finesse. Within this chapter, we'll venture into the realm of customizing user permissions and group-based access control, delving into the technical intricacies while showcasing their practical application in real-world scenarios.

Delving into User Permissions:

User permissions serve as the foundation of application security and functionality. They dictate the actions a user can undertake within the application, such as creating, editing, or deleting content. Django's permission system is both sophisticated and user-friendly, providing developers the ability to define permissions on models and manage access rights with meticulous precision.

Permission Definition in Django:

Django offers a straightforward yet potent method for defining permissions using the permissions attribute within model classes.

python

```python
from django.db import models

class Article(models.Model):
    title = models.CharField(max_length=200)
    content = models.TextField()

    class Meta:
        permissions = [
            ("can_publish", "Can publish articles"),
            ("can_edit", "Can edit articles"),
        ]
```

In this illustration, we define two customized permissions: can_publish and can_edit. These permissions can be allocated to user groups to regulate their access to specific actions.

Group-Centric Access Governance:

As applications develop, overseeing consents independently for each client can ended up cumbersome. Django's group-based get to control offers an exquisite arrangement. Clients are gathered, and consents are credited to these bunches, instead of to person clients.

python

```python
from django.contrib.auth.models import Group

# Creating a group
editor_group = Group.objects.create(name='Editors')

# Allocating permissions to the group
editor_group.permissions.add(Permission.objects.get(cod
ename='can_publish'))
```

In this excerpt, we establish an Editors group and allocate the can_publish permission to it. Consequently, any user affiliated with the Editors group inherits the associated permissions.

Real-World Implementation:

Consider a content management system where users assume roles like authors, editors, and administrators. Authors possess the ability to craft content, editors can publish and modify, while administrators command full control. By configuring permissions aptly and segmenting users into respective groups, the system fosters an organized editorial process while upholding security.

Precision Control with Decorators:

Django's decorators emerge as a potent tool for access control. They permit developers to restrict access to specific views based on user permissions.

python

```
from django.contrib.auth.decorators import
permission_required

@permission_required('can_publish')
def publish_article(request, article_id):
    # Logic to publish the article
```

In this scenario, the publish_article view is accessible only to users with the can_publish permission. If a user without the requisite permission seeks to access this view, access will be denied.

Access Audit through Middleware:

Django's middleware can be harnessed to log and scrutinize user actions, a valuable asset in situations where accountability and traceability take precedence.

Striking a Harmonious Balance:

While Django's access control features offer vast flexibility, maintaining a harmonious equilibrium between user permissions and security is paramount. Excessive permissions can lead to data breaches, whereas overly restrictive access might impede user efficiency.

Concluding Reflections:

Customizing user permissions and group-based access control within Django bestows developers with the means to mold application security and functionality with finesse. By delineating permissions, establishing user groups, and leveraging decorators and middleware, developers can shape access rights in alignment with user roles. In an era where data integrity and user trust are paramount, mastering these techniques enables developers to craft applications that concurrently empower users and safeguard sensitive data. Proficiency in access control equips developers to ensure that individuals wield appropriate access levels, reinforcing application integrity and augmenting user experiences.

Building a robust and secure user management system

Within the intricate realm of web application development, establishing a resilient and secure user management system emerges as a cornerstone of triumph. At the core of user experiences and application security lies the delicate orchestration of user accounts, authentication, and authorization. To navigate this domain, Django, a versatile web framework, furnishes an array of tools and methodologies that empower developers to create a user management system not only marked by seamless user interactions but fortified against potential threats. In the following discourse, we delve deep into the inner workings of shaping an impervious user management system, one that embodies both strength and security.

Recognizing the Significance:

The essence of a user management system transcends mere functionality, as it encompasses the orchestration of account creation, authentication, password maintenance, and access control. As custodians of sensitive user data, nurturing its robustness and security stands paramount in fostering trust and safeguarding vital information.

Laying the Groundwork with the User Model:

At the heart of the Django user management ecosystem lies the pivotal user model. This model furnishes the bedrock for user-oriented operations, endowed with vital attributes and functions for user accounts. While Django's native User model serves as a robust starting point, for tailored exigencies, extending this model or implementing a bespoke user model unveils itself as an advantageous trajectory.

python

```python
from django.contrib.auth.models import AbstractUser

class CustomUser(AbstractUser):
    # Additional fields and methods
```

The 'AbstractUser' extension blueprint empowers developers to append supplementary fields and methods to the user model, infusing it with tailor-made attributes to suit the application's distinct requisites.

The Tandem of Authentication and Authorization:

Authentication and authorization forge the heart of any user management system. Django's steadfast authentication system flexes its prowess through a spectrum of authentication backends, encompassing conventional username/password, email/password, and the realm of social authentication.

python

```python
from django.contrib.auth import authenticate, login, logout

user = authenticate(username='username', password='password')
if user:
    login(request, user)
else:
    # Authentication failed
```

Once authenticated, the authorization arm steps in, dictating that users have access solely to resources they are lawfully permitted to interact with. The incorporation of Django's inbuilt permission system, coupled with decorators, underpins this process.

A Sentinel for Password Security:

Passwords, those digital sentinels, safeguard the gateway to user security. Django champions the deployment of robust hashing algorithms, coupled with salt encryption, to house passwords securely. By advocating stringent password protocols and incorporating mechanisms for password resets, the user management system reinforces its security fortress.

The Dual-Factor Symphony:

Elevating the security echelon involves implementing two-factor authentication (2FA). Django harmonizes this endeavor with external packages like 'django-two-factor-auth', facilitating the seamless integration of 2FA into the user management fabric.

Navigating User Registration and Profile Management:

User registration interfaces often herald the initial point of interaction. Django's form framework expedites the creation of user registration forms, endowing them with validation and error-handling resilience.

python

```python
from django import forms
from django.contrib.auth.forms import UserCreationForm

class RegistrationForm(UserCreationForm):
    # Additional fields and customizations
```

Accompanying this is profile management, emboldening users to administer their data, trigger password modifications, and manipulate email preferences, rendering user engagement seamless.

Dismantling Accounts and Data Retention:

In line with contemporary privacy tenets and user expectations, introducing mechanisms for account suspension and data retention emerges as a prudent step. Affording users the authority to suspend accounts and exercise data retention prerogatives enhances transparency and aligns with regulatory requisites.

Fending Off Security Incursions:

Upholding a user management system's fortitude necessitates a robust defense against security threats, encompassing SQL injections, cross-site scripting (XSS), cross-site request forgery (CSRF), and brute-force onslaughts. Utilizing Django's innate safeguards, validating user inputs, and adhering to the doctrine of secure coding collectively fortify the system against these vulnerabilities.

Third-Party Authentication and Single Sign-On (SSO):

To amalgamate seamlessness with security, grafting third-party authentication gateways (such as Google or Facebook) and integrating the expanse of Single Sign-On (SSO) can elevate user interactions while bolstering the protective perimeter.

Documenting Audit Trails and Orchestrating Logs:

Incorporating audit trails and logging user actions ushers in an indispensable tool for tracking shifts and identifying irregularities. Django's versatile logging framework stands primed to chronicle these actions.

In the Light of Data Encryption and GDPR Compliance:

For applications entrusted with sensitive user data, encoding data and embracing General Data Protection Regulation (GDPR) mandates loom as prerequisites. These measures harness security and establish compliance in the same breath.

The creation of a potent and secure user management system stands as a keystone in the art of web application development. By fashioning a meticulously designed user model, assimilating robust authentication and authorization protocols, addressing password integrity, and contemplating advanced facets like two-factor authentication and third-party integration, developers summon forth a user management system that not only heightens user experiences but also safeguards the core of the application's security. With a dedication to security precepts and a commitment to user privacy, developers render the user data impregnable and furnish users with the confidence to interact with the application in a secure environment.

Chapter Seven

Full-Text Search with Django and Elasticsearch

Integrating Elasticsearch for efficient and accurate full-text search

In the dynamic sphere of modern web applications, the ability to swiftly and precisely navigate vast textual datasets has surged to the forefront as a pivotal attribute. This is where Elasticsearch steps onto the stage—a distributed, open-source engine for search and analytics that has redefined the landscape of full-text exploration. In the upcoming chapter, we embark on a journey to seamlessly integrate Elasticsearch into Django applications, uncovering its capability to elevate search efficiency to unprecedented heights while delivering laser-focused accuracy.

Unveiling the Essence of Elasticsearch:

Elasticsearch transcends the boundaries of a mere search engine; it stands as a powerhouse for managing textual data with unparalleled finesse. Its prowess spans indexing, search operations, and real-time data analytics. The engine's adeptness in executing intricate queries, encompassing nuanced elements like fuzzy matching and relevance ranking, underscores its role as a potent ally in conquering the intricacies of full-text exploration.

The Art of Integration:

Bridging the realms of Django and Elasticsearch is accomplished primarily through the acclaimed Django REST framework. By embracing the django-elasticsearch-dsl library, developers can seamlessly align Django models with Elasticsearch indexes, fostering a harmonious synthesis.

python

```python
from elasticsearch_dsl import Document, Text

class BlogIndex(Document):
    title = Text()
    content = Text()

    class Index:
        name = 'blog_index'
```

The BlogIndex document model mirrors the architecture of the corresponding Blog model in Django. The Index class elucidates the appellation for the Elasticsearch index housing the meticulously indexed data.

Indexing Unveiled:

Elasticsearch's might unfurls through the process of data indexing. In the Django environment, indexing assumes form via the creation of documents that mirror the underlying models. These documents encapsulate the essence of data destined for inclusion in Elasticsearch.

python

```
from elasticsearch_dsl import Index

blog_index = Index('blog_index')
blog_index.document(BlogIndex)
```

Navigating the Realm of Searches:

Elasticsearch's prowess in search unfurls through its robust querying mechanisms. The Search object unfetters the ability to shape intricate queries that transcend the boundaries of simple keyword matches.

python

```
from elasticsearch_dsl import Search

s = Search(index='blog_index').query('match',
title='Elasticsearch')
response = s.execute()

for hit in response:
    print(hit.title)
```

In this illustration, a straightforward query is constructed to match documents featuring the term 'Elasticsearch' within their titles. Elasticsearch's query capabilities span a spectrum, including facets like phrase matching, range queries, and fuzzy matching.

Autocomplete and Faceted Search Realized:

The realm of Elasticsearch surpasses basic text matching, extending its dominion to include dynamic attributes like autocomplete and faceted search. The Autocomplete feature, propelled by Elasticsearch's Suggest API, equips developers to deliver rapid suggestions based on user input.

python

```python
from elasticsearch_dsl import Completion

class BlogIndex(Document):
    title = Text()
    content = Text()
    suggest = Completion()

    class Index:
        name = 'blog_index'
```

The addition of the suggest field infuses the system with the capacity to furnish autocomplete suggestions based on users' inputs.

Augmenting Search Efficiency:

Elevating search efficiency to its zenith is a goal well within reach, courtesy of Elasticsearch's tuning opportunities. The manipulation of index settings, mappings, and analyzers unfurls a panorama of potentialities for optimizing search outcomes. By harnessing the prowess of Elasticsearch's analyzers, developers can fine-tune the tokenization and indexing of textual content to perfection.

Scaling the Heights:

As data volumes escalate, the significance of a scalable, distributed architecture becomes paramount. Elasticsearch's distributed character equips it to seamlessly navigate colossal datasets across multiple nodes. The architecture's pillars of clustering, sharding, and replication safeguard high availability and resilience against failures.

By seamlessly intertwining Elasticsearch into Django applications, developers open doors to a new dimension of possibilities in the realm of full-text exploration. Its efficiency, versatility, and advanced query capabilities empower developers to sculpt search experiences that transcend the confines of rudimentary keyword matches. From data indexing to intricate searches, the integration of features like autocomplete and performance optimization empowers Elasticsearch to redefine our interaction with textual data. Through the orchestration of its capabilities, developers not only amplify search efficiency but also bestow upon users search outcomes characterized by paramount precision and relevance.

Implementing autocomplete and faceted search features

Making effective and user-friendly look functionalities is of foremost significance in today's fast-paced computerized scene. Improving client involvement through progressed look highlights, such as autocomplete and faceted look, can altogether hoist the quality of web applications. In this segment, we'll dig into the complexities of joining these advanced look capabilities into Django applications.

Enabling Autocomplete Search

Autocomplete look, moreover alluded to as type-ahead look, predicts and proposes look terms to clients as they sort within the look bar. This highlight improves client involvement by giving quick and exact look recommendations, viably decreasing the time required to total a look inquiry. In the context of Django, implementing autocomplete search can be achieved through various techniques, with one prominent approach involving the utilization of Elasticsearch—an open-source search and analytics engine that empowers efficient search functionalities.

Configuring Elasticsearch

The initial step in implementing autocomplete search involves the setup of Elasticsearch and its seamless integration into your Django project. To begin, install the elasticsearch-dsl package, which equips you with a high-level library for Python-based interactions with Elasticsearch.

bash

```
pip install elasticsearch-dsl
```

Subsequently, adjust your settings.py to configure your Django project to utilize Elasticsearch as the search backend.

python

```python
ELASTICSEARCH_DSL = {
    'default': {
        'hosts': 'localhost:9200',  # Update with your
Elasticsearch server's address
    },
}
```

Indexing Data

For effective autocomplete, creating an Elasticsearch index housing the relevant search data is imperative. Let's consider a scenario wherein autocomplete is applied to a model named Product. Within your Django app's search_indexes.py, define an Elasticsearch index tailored for the model.

python

```python
from elasticsearch_dsl import Document, Text

class ProductIndex(Document):
    name = Text()

    class Index:
        name = 'product_index'

    def prepare_name(self, instance):
        return instance.name
```

Here, the prepare_name function designates the field to be employed for autocomplete purposes. It is vital to ensure that the indexed data is aptly curated to offer swift and pertinent autocomplete suggestions.

Autocomplete View

Forge a view within your Django app to facilitate autocomplete suggestions. In your views.py:

python

```
from elasticsearch_dsl import Q
from elasticsearch_dsl.query import MultiMatch
from django.http import JsonResponse
from .models import Product
from .search_indexes import ProductIndex

def autocomplete_view(request):
    term = request.GET.get('term', '')
    search = ProductIndex.search().query(
        MultiMatch(query=term, fields=['name'],
type='phrase_prefix')
    )
    results = search.execute()
    suggestions = [hit.name for hit in results.hits]
    return JsonResponse(suggestions, safe=False)
```

In this instance, the autocomplete_view receives a search term via a GET request parameter. It queries the Elasticsearch index for suggestions utilizing a phrase_prefix search, a method particularly adept at catering to autocomplete scenarios.

Incorporating Autocomplete into the UI

The final step involves embedding the autocomplete functionality into your frontend through JavaScript libraries such as jQuery UI or Autocomplete.js. Attach an event listener to your search input field to trigger the retrieval and display of autocomplete suggestions originating from the Django view.

Realizing Faceted Search

Faceted search, also known as guided navigation, empowers users to refine search outcomes using a selection of filters often presented as facets. This functionality is invaluable for e-commerce platforms and applications housing substantial data repositories. In Django, accomplishing faceted search is facilitated through Elasticsearch's aggregation capabilities.

Indexing Facets

To implement faceted search, additional fields corresponding to the desired facets should be indexed within your Elasticsearch index. For instance, in the context of an e-commerce platform, facets like "Category," "Brand," and "Price Range" could be offered.

python

```python
class ProductIndex(Document):
    name = Text()
    category = Text(fields={'raw': Keyword()})
    brand = Text(fields={'raw': Keyword()})
    price = Float()

    # ... other fields and methods ...
```

Within this illustration, facets such as category, brand, and price are indexed. The raw field is employed for precise keyword matching, while the primary field facilitates full-text search.

Faceted Search View

Generate a view responsible for handling faceted search queries and aggregations. Refine your views.py:

python

```python
def faceted_search_view(request):
    category_filter = request.GET.get('category', '')
    brand_filter = request.GET.get('brand', '')
    price_filter = request.GET.get('price', '')

    search = ProductIndex.search()

    if category_filter:
        search = search.filter('term',
category=category_filter)
    if brand_filter:
        search = search.filter('term',
brand=brand_filter)
    if price_filter:
        min_price, max_price = price_filter.split('-')
        search = search.filter('range', price={'gte':
min_price, 'lte': max_price})

    response = search.execute()
    results = [hit.name for hit in response.hits]
    return JsonResponse(results, safe=False)
```

Within this view, the chosen user filters are processed, and the Elasticsearch index is queried accordingly. The filters can be combined to efficiently narrow down search outcomes.

Introducing Faceted Search to the UI

On the frontend, devise a user interface that showcases facets and allows users to select filters. As users interact with the filters, perform AJAX requests to the Django view, which, in turn, delivers updated search results grounded in the chosen facets.

The integration of autocomplete and faceted search functionalities into Django applications can significantly

105

augment user experience and engagement. Leveraging Elasticsearch and its advanced search capabilities empowers you to present users with instantaneous search suggestions and finely tuned search results. With a well-implemented autocomplete and faceted search, your Django application can provide a robust and intuitive search experience that fosters user loyalty and satisfaction.

Optimizing search performance and scalability

Enhancing the efficiency and scalability of search operations within Django applications is a vital pursuit in the contemporary landscape of web applications. As data volumes expand and user expectations intensify, the optimization of search performance becomes pivotal. In this segment, we will delve into strategies that elevate the swiftness and scalability of search processes in Django applications.

Indexing and Data Modeling

The foundation of optimized search lies in the meticulous indexing and modeling of data. Elasticsearch, a potent search engine, stores data in a format that is meticulously optimized, ensuring swift retrieval. To establish an ideal indexing approach, consider the following measures:

1. Prudent Field Selection for Indexing

Prioritize fields pivotal for search and filtering. Emphasize textual content like product names, descriptions, and tags. For numeric values, such as prices, opt for Elasticsearch's numeric data types, which bolster the efficiency of range queries.

2. Harnessing Analyzers and Tokenizers

Unleash the potential of Elasticsearch's analyzers and tokenizers for pre-processing text prior to indexing. These tools dissect text into distinct terms, enabling nuanced and efficient searches. Customize analyzers to harmonize with the linguistic attributes of your data.

3. The Power of Denormalization

Incorporate denormalization to encompass correlated data within a singular document. This reduces the demand for intricate joins during search queries, which translates to accelerated retrieval times. Yet, temper denormalization with considerations for data consistency.

Optimization of Queries

Strategically formulating queries is pivotal to search performance. Elasticsearch's query DSL provides a potent array of tools to craft intricate queries that retrieve pertinent outcomes with expediency.

1. Harnessing Match and Multi-Match Queries

Employ the match query for full-text searches targeting specific fields. The multi_match query extends the search scope across multiple fields concurrently. For heightened relevance, contemplate elevating certain fields to exert influence over result ranking.

2. The Significance of Filters and Aggregations

Deploy filters to narrow down search outcomes based on particular criteria. Filters are cached, thereby enhancing performance for repetitive queries with akin filters. Aggregations yield insights into data distribution and enable the generation of summaries, histograms, and more.

The Power of Caching

Caching emerges as a potent technique to alleviate the load on the search infrastructure, particularly for queries that encounter frequent execution.

1. Caching of Query Outcomes

Cache query outcomes that experience frequent requests, thus alleviating the burden on the search engine. Tools such as Redis or Memcached can house outcomes, which subsequently are furnished directly from the cache for subsequent identical queries.

2. Caching of Field Data

Elasticsearch's caching of field data retains frequently accessed field values within memory. This sharpens the speed of aggregations and sorting. Exercise vigilance in monitoring memory consumption and configuring cache settings to align with optimal performance.

Sharding and Replication

As data accumulates, embracing sharding and replication strategies is pivotal to ensure scalability and the fortification of Elasticsearch.

1. Embracing Sharding

Fragment your index into smaller units referred to as shards, which can be dispersed across multiple nodes. Sharding orchestrates load equilibrium, facilitates parallel search operations, and aligns with horizontal expansion endeavors.

2. The Role of Replication

Replication engenders replicas of shards, distributing data across nodes to deliver redundancy and elevated availability. It also augments read performance by rendering requests from replicas, thus diminishing the load on the primary shard.

Monitoring and Scaling

Uninterrupted monitoring stands as a linchpin in upholding search performance throughout the evolution of your application.

1. The Arsenal of Monitoring Tools

Harness the built-in monitoring and diagnostic instruments furnished by Elasticsearch to oversee resource consumption, query performance, and index health. Supplementary tools like Kibana proffer visualizations and dashboards for enriched insights.

2. The Saga of Scaling

When search traffic experiences surges, scaling emerges as a necessity. Vertical scaling entails elevating hardware resources, whereas horizontal scaling encompasses the addition of nodes to the Elasticsearch cluster. The incorporation of load balancers ensures even traffic distribution.

A Culmination of Insights

The elevation of search performance and scalability in Django applications embodies a multifaceted venture that demands meticulous contemplation of data modeling, query optimization, caching techniques, and infrastructure scaling. By tapping into the capabilities of Elasticsearch and adhering to established best practices, you can ensure that your search functionality maintains its agility, reliability, and ability to accommodate the burgeoning demands of users. Regular monitoring, refinements, and preemptive scaling initiatives contribute to nurturing a superlative search experience that not only gratifies users but also stimulates sustained engagement.

Chapter Eight

Advanced Caching Strategies

Utilizing caching for improving application performance

Elevating the performance of web applications stands as an unceasing goal within contemporary web development. An effective ally in achieving this objective is caching—a technique that stores frequently accessed data in a readily accessible state, thereby mitigating the demands of fetching information. In this section, we'll delve into the significance of caching and explore methodologies for employing it to bolster the performance of your applications.

Grasping Caching's Essence

Caching serves as a potent approach to tackle the performance hurdles commonly encountered during data retrieval and computation. Rather than engaging in repetitive data fetching or recalculating identical outcomes, caching conserves time and computational resources by stockpiling these results for swift access. This proves especially beneficial for data characterized by stability over time or entailing resource-intensive processing.

Diverse Caching Approaches

Numerous caching strategies are available, each tailored to distinct scenarios and aims:

1. Page Caching: This strategy entails caching entire HTML pages, ready to be directly served to users. Page caching is particularly apt for content that remains unchanging across various user interactions.

2. Object Caching: Object caching revolves around caching frequently accessed objects or data structures. This approach shines when data retrieval incurs resource-intensive efforts.

3. Query Caching: This variant centers on caching the outcomes of database queries, trimming the overhead of recurrent querying for identical data.

4. Fragment Caching: Here, specific portions of a page are cached, permitting the caching of dynamic content while retaining the flexibility to refresh other elements.

Enacting Caching in Django

Within the Django framework, caching integrates seamlessly, rendering it effortless for developers to optimize application performance.

1. Caching Setup: Commence by configuring caching settings within your Django project's settings.py file. A variety of caching backends, encompassing memory-based choices like Memcached or file-based alternatives, are at your disposal.

python

```
CACHES = {
    'default': {
        'BACKEND':
'django.core.cache.backends.memcached.MemcachedCache',
        'LOCATION': '127.0.0.1:11211',
    }
}
```

2. View-Level Caching: You have the prerogative to apply caching to specific views through decorators, ensuring that the output of these views is cached and furnished to subsequent users sans recalculations.

python

```python
from django.views.decorators.cache import cache_page

@cache_page(60 * 15)  # Cache the page for 15 minutes
def cached_view(request):
    # Your view logic here
```

3. Template Fragment Caching: Within templates, targeted portions of content can be cached using template tags. This proves ideal for scenarios where only select segments of a page exhibit dynamism.

html

```html
{% load cache %}

{% cache 600 "my_cache_key" %}
<p>This content will be cached for 10 minutes.</p>
{% endcache %}
```

Cache Invalidation and Lifespan

While caching exerts a considerable impact on performance, maintaining equilibrium between caching and data freshness is paramount. Outdated or inaccurate data can undermine the user experience.

1. Cache Invalidation: Deploy mechanisms to automatically invalidate or update cached content as underlying data undergoes modifications. This could involve manual cache

clearance post updates or the adoption of cache tags to invalidate clusters of interrelated items.

2. Cache Lifespan: Set appropriate cache expiration periods contingent on the frequency of data alterations. Brief expiration times warrant data precision but might elevate cache miss instances, while prolonged durations raise the prospect of dispensing outdated content.

Caching Tactics for Scalability

Caching assumes a pivotal role in bolstering application scalability. It alleviates the strain on databases and other backend services, contributing to smoother user experiences and judicious resource utilization.

1. Content Delivery Networks (CDNs): Incorporating CDNs facilitates the caching and dispersion of static assets—like images, stylesheets, and JavaScript files. CDNs expedite content delivery by rendering these assets accessible from servers situated in closer proximity to users.

2. Edge Caching: Edge caching takes center stage, caching content at the network's edge, diminishing the latency between users' browsers and servers. This proves notably efficacious for global applications catering to diverse user locations.

Caching emerges as a potent means to elevate application performance, ushering in rapidity and responsiveness—an expectation that users hold in high regard. Through skillful incorporation of caching methodologies within your Django applications, you can substantially pare down data retrieval and processing overheads. Nonetheless, it's imperative to strike a balance between caching and data timeliness, navigating the realm of cache invalidation and expiry with finesse. Ultimately, a meticulously devised caching strategy not only culminates in immediate performance enhancements but also bolsters the scalability and dependability of your applications.

Implementing cache partitions and fine-grained caching

In the realm of optimizing web application performance, the integration of sophisticated caching tactics takes center stage. Among these, the utilization of cache partitions and fine-grained caching emerges as a strategic maneuver, conferring meticulous control over data storage and retrieval. In this segment, we'll delve into the paramount significance of these tactics and explore their application to garner peak performance enhancements.

Decoding Cache Partitions

Cache partitions encompass the segregation of cached data into distinct segments, each devoted to a specific data subset. This partitioning strategy imparts an elevated level of cache management, enabling precision actions on subsets, curtailing cache clashes, and amplifying cache hit rates. Cache partitions find their niche particularly in scenarios where data unveils diverse access patterns and varying degrees of volatility.

Enacting Cache Partitions

To put cache partitions into action, let's consider a hypothetical scenario in an e-commerce application where products span diverse categories. The goal is to engineer cache partitions for individual product categories, ensuring that any modifications to one category remain insulated from the others.

python

```python
from django.core.cache import cache

def get_products_by_category(category_id):
    cached_products =
cache.get(f'category_{category_id}_products')

    if cached_products is None:
        products =
Product.objects.filter(category=category_id)
        cache.set(f'category_{category_id}_products',
products)
        return products

    return cached_products
```

In this illustration, products affiliated with a distinct category are cached with a distinct key encompassing the category's identifier. This judiciously isolates products on a categorical basis, precluding the reverberations of alterations in one category on the others.

The Intricacies of Fine-Grained Caching

Fine-grained caching elevates the cache partitioning paradigm, permitting caching at the minutiae level of individual objects or components. This approach refines cache deployment by confining caching to specific data fragments that undergo frequent access or entail computational intricacies. Fine-grained caching shines in scenarios where particular data elements undergo more frequent changes than others.

The Application of Fine-Grained Caching

Picture an application spotlighting client profiles. Inside this setting, rather than caching whole client profiles, fine-grained caching enters the shred, empowering the caching of particular attributes—such as the user's title and profile picture.

python

```python
def get_user_profile(user_id):
    cached_name = cache.get(f'user_{user_id}_name')
    cached_avatar = cache.get(f'user_{user_id}_avatar')

    if cached_name and cached_avatar:
        return {'name': cached_name, 'avatar': cached_avatar}

    user = User.objects.get(pk=user_id)
    cache.set(f'user_{user_id}_name', user.name)
    cache.set(f'user_{user_id}_avatar', user.avatar)

    return {'name': user.name, 'avatar': user.avatar}
```

In this occasion, the user's title and profile picture are cached freely. Should either attribute undergo alteration, only the pertinent cache entry faces invalidation, keeping the unchanged attribute's cached value intact.

The Dance of Precision and Complexity

While cache partitions and fine-grained caching usher in substantial performance rewards, they also introduce intricacy. Striking a harmonious equilibrium between precision and manageability is the crux. Fine-grained caching might potentially yield a profusion of cache entries and elevated cache management overhead. Prudent analysis of data access patterns, volatility, and the cadence of modifications guides decisions pertaining to which components merit individual caching.

Wrapping Up

Integration of cache partitions and fine-grained caching presents an avenue to fine-tune web application performance by customizing caching tactics to data access patterns and volatility. Cache partitions enable data segmentation into manageable segments, trimming cache clashes, and heightening cache hit rates. Fine-grained caching, in turn, elevates this by permitting the caching of specific fragments or attributes. As with any caching approach, attaining an equilibrium between precision and intricacy is key. By proficiently integrating these advanced caching methodologies within your Django applications, you can harvest substantial performance improvements and furnish users with an unparalleled experience.

Cache invalidation and handling cache-related issues

Mastering cache invalidation and adroitly addressing cache-related intricacies constitute integral domains within the tapestry of web application development. However, the concept of cache invalidation and the finesse demanded by managing cache-related complexities beckon a closer inspection. In this exposition, we will delve into the heart of cache invalidation and proffer strategies for skillfully navigating the multifaceted realm of cache-related challenges.

Unraveling the Essence of Cache Invalidation

Cache invalidation, at its core, signifies the strategic process of expunging or rejuvenating cached data to align it with the most up-to-date and accurate information. Stale or outdated cache entries bear the potential to undermine user experience and jeopardize data consistency. Cache invalidation acts as the safeguard against the propagation of erroneous information, curbing misinformed decisions, and nurturing the sanctity of data accuracy.

Navigating Techniques for Cache Invalidation

Efficient cache invalidation strategies are the linchpin to sustaining data precision. Multiple methodologies can be harnessed to steer seamless cache invalidation:

1. Time-Based Expiry:

Infuse cached items with an expiration timestamp, triggering automatic invalidation and refresh once a predetermined time interval elapses. This strategy finds its mettle when data anticipates changes at predefined junctures.

python

```python
from django.core.cache import cache

def cache_data():
    data = fetch_data_from_database()
    cache.set('cached_data', data, timeout=3600)   #
Cache for 1 hour

def retrieve_data():
    cached_data = cache.get('cached_data')
    if cached_data is None:
```

```
        cached_data = fetch_data_from_database()
        cache.set('cached_data', cached_data,
timeout=3600)
    return cached_data
```

2. Event-Driven Invalidation:

Trigger cache invalidation in the wake of updates to associated data. This can be accomplished through signals or hooks primed to react to data mutations.

python

```python
from django.core.cache import cache
from django.db.models.signals import post_save
from django.dispatch import receiver

@receiver(post_save, sender=Product)
def invalidate_product_cache(sender, instance,
**kwargs):
    cache.delete(f'product_{instance.id}')
```

3. Manual Invalidation:

Explicitly invalidate cache entries based on specific events or triggers. This method confers meticulous control over when cache entries are nullified.

python

```python
from django.core.cache import cache

def update_product_price(product_id, new_price):
    product = Product.objects.get(pk=product_id)
    product.price = new_price
    product.save()
```

```
cache.delete(f'product_{product_id}')
```

Adeptly Confronting Cache-Related Challenges

While caching reaps considerable performance rewards, it simultaneously unfurls complexities necessitating judicious management. Several challenges merit vigilant consideration:

1. Cache Consistency:

Upholding congruence between cached data and the database assumes paramount significance. Approaches such as transactional cache updates ensure data alterations reverberate uniformly across cached and persistent data realms.

2. Cache Stampede:

The simultaneous expiration of caches—referred to as a cache stampede—can place undue strain on resources during cache regeneration. Mitigation is possible through the employment of cache locks or utilization of cache keys that remain valid during the refresh process.

3. Cache Warming:

Instances like application startups or cache flushes can usher in a volley of requests seeking to replenish the cache, potentially exerting an impact on server performance. Tackling this challenge necessitates deploying cache warming techniques during off-peak intervals to prudently repopulate the cache.

Navigating Cache Invalidation with Delicacy

Mastery over cache invalidation unfolds as a nuanced skill, underpinned by a robust comprehension of data access patterns, update frequencies, and user interactions. The fusion of time-based expiry, event-driven invalidation, and manual invalidation can orchestrate a balanced cache management strategy. Nonetheless, diligent surveillance of cache behavior, tracking cache hit rates, and judicious recalibration of strategies as application dynamics evolve remain imperative.

Cache invalidation and the finesse required for addressing cache-related challenges emerge as vital domains for web application developers endeavoring to optimize performance while preserving data integrity. Through astutely honed cache invalidation techniques, the scourge of data incongruities can be vanquished, safeguarding user experiences and facilitating informed choices. By adroitly navigating the labyrinthine terrain of cache management, encompassing cache consistency, cache stampedes, and cache warming, developers can architect a cache strategy that not only elevates performance but also upholds the sanctity of data precision.

Chapter Nine

Designing and Implementing Scalable Architecture

Planning and architecting scalable Django applications

Navigating the intricacies of building scalable Django applications emerges as a pivotal endeavor within the realm of web development. The architecture underpinning an application constitutes the bedrock upon which its scalability rests. For Django applications poised to embrace increasing user demands and surges in system load, meticulous planning and astute architectural decisions become the cornerstones for establishing a resilient and scalable framework. In this discourse, we shall delve into the essence of strategizing and crafting scalable Django applications, accompanied by pragmatic insights and strategies for executing this vision with finesse.

Grasping Scalability within Django's Domain

Scalability, at its essence, revolves around an application's capacity to gracefully accommodate amplified user loads and burgeoning demands while upholding peak performance and responsiveness. In the context of the Django framework, achieving scalability mandates a comprehensive approach that encompasses both vertical and horizontal scaling.

Vertical Scaling:

Vertical scaling entails boosting an application's performance by elevating the resources allocated to a single server instance. This could encompass upgrading hardware components such as CPU, memory, and storage. While vertical scaling proffers immediate performance enhancements, its limitations are often tethered to the ultimate capacity of a solitary server.

Horizontal Scaling:

Horizontal scaling takes a distributed stance by integrating additional servers into the application ecosystem. This is accomplished via load balancing methodologies that uniformly distribute incoming requests across numerous server instances. Horizontal scaling assumes a pivotal role in accommodating swift expansion and spikes in user traffic.

Architecting Scalable Django Applications: A Blueprint

Shepherding the creation of a scalable Django application unfolds as a sequence of strategic phases spanning architecture, database management, and the distribution of load. Presented below is a blueprint to steer your endeavors:

1. Database Optimization:

A robust database blueprint constitutes the nucleus of scalability. Employ database normalization techniques, opt for apt indexes, and selectively embrace denormalization to strike equilibrium between read and write operations. Venture into the sphere of Django's inherent ORM (Object-Relational Mapping) to streamline interactions with databases.

2. Caching Strategies:

Harness the prowess of caching to unburden database queries and data that experiences recurrent access. Deploy page-level caching, object caching, and query caching with precision to truncate redundant computations. Leverage the cache partitioning and fine-grained caching tactics discussed earlier to extract optimal performance.

3. Load Balancing:

Disseminate incoming traffic across manifold server instances utilizing load balancers. Noteworthy load balancing options encompass NGINX, HAProxy, and cloud-based load balancers. The ripple effect of load balancing isn't confined to bolstering response times; it seamlessly ushers in scalability through the integration of new servers.

4. Database Sharding:

In instances where a solitary database instance morphs into a bottleneck, the avenue of database sharding beckons. Sharding delves into partitioning data across diverse database instances, thereby fostering horizontal scaling of database resources. However, the pursuit of sharding mandates calculated forethought and meticulous planning.

5. Asynchronous Processing:

Infuse asynchronous programming and task queues into the fabric of your application to tackle resource-intensive and time-elongated operations. Tools like Celery can be enmeshed to oversee background tasks, thereby freeing server resources for more instantaneous user demands.

6. Microservices Architecture:

Contemplate embracing a microservices architectural blueprint wherein distinct components of your application are sculpted and released as independent services. This approach empowers the scaling of individual services in accordance with demand while expediting maintenance and updates.

Code Example: Load Balancing with NGINX

Here's a code snippet illuminating the establishment of load balancing through NGINX, serving as a reverse proxy:

nginx

```
http {
    upstream django_app {
        server app_server1;
        server app_server2;
        # Incorporate more server instances as deemed
necessary
    }

    server {
        listen 80;
        server_name example.com;

        location / {
            proxy_pass http://django_app;
        }
    }
}
```

The expedition towards crafting scalable Django applications hinges on a multidimensional symphony of architectural selections, database optimization, caching strategies, load balancing, and beyond. By adroitly maneuvering through this landscape, you pave the way for an application poised to seamlessly accommodate surges in user requisites while consistently delivering optimal performance. Through a judicious interplay of vertical and horizontal scaling, coupled with astute architectural determinations, you chart a course towards cultivating a rugged and scalable Django ecosystem adeptly primed to surmount the challenges of today's dynamic digital panorama.

Load balancing, caching, and optimizing database performance

Navigating the landscape of web application optimization, the trio of load balancing, caching, and enhancing database performance emerges as a formidable alliance. This union equips applications with the robustness and efficiency required to tackle rising user demands while ensuring seamless user experiences. This discourse delves deep into the complexities of load balancing, caching, and optimizing database performance, demystifying their significance and delving into the intricacies of their application.

Orchestrating Load Balancing for Resilience

Load balancing is the practice of evenly distributing incoming traffic across multiple server instances, fostering equilibrium and preventing any single server from bearing an excessive load. This technique enhances the application's reliability, optimally utilizes resources, and paves the way for scalability in the face of escalating user demands.

Code Illustration: Load Balancing with NGINX

nginx

```
http {
    upstream app_servers {
        server server1;
        server server2;
        # Incorporate more server instances as needed
    }

    server {
        listen 80;
        server_name example.com;

        location / {
            proxy_pass http://app_servers;
        }
    }
}
```

Harnessing Caching for Stellar Performance

Caching, an indispensable facet of performance optimization, revolves around storing frequently accessed data in a dedicated cache. By expediting data retrieval and alleviating server processing, caching curtails repetitive computations and boosts response times. A gamut of caching strategies, from page-level caching to object caching, can be tailored to suit specific application requisites.

Implementation of Caching Strategies

Incorporating caching strategies demands meticulous reflection on the data type, its volatility, and the patterns of access. Page-level caching conserves complete HTML pages, while object caching focuses on stashing frequently queried database results or computed data. The toolkit encompasses utilities like Django's caching framework, empowering developers to selectively cache data components.

Elevating Database Performance through Optimization

Database performance optimization assumes a pivotal stance within this triumvirate. A finely tuned database forms the bedrock of application speed and responsiveness. Strategies encompass indexing, query optimization, database normalization, and astute utilization of denormalization to balance the scales between read and write operations.

Code Illustration: Database Indexing

python

```python
class Product(models.Model):
    name = models.CharField(max_length=100)
    category = models.ForeignKey(Category,
on_delete=models.CASCADE)
    price = models.DecimalField(max_digits=10,
decimal_places=2)

    class Meta:
        indexes = [
            models.Index(fields=['name']),
            models.Index(fields=['category']),
        ]
```

Navigating the Nexus with Expertise

Navigating the synergistic interplay of load balancing, caching, and database optimization necessitates finesse in both planning and execution. Load balancing for resilience ensures that the weight is uniformly distributed, safeguarding against server strain. Caching expedites data retrieval and database optimization fine-tunes data access, together culminating in enhanced overall application performance.

Striking an Equilibrium

While each component of this triad contributes uniquely to application performance, their harmonious integration hinges on striking equilibrium. Load balancing, caching, and database optimization must be woven into the fabric of the application holistically, accounting for unique needs, traffic patterns, and resource availability.

The convergence of load balancing, caching, and database performance enhancement stands as the cornerstone of constructing web applications poised to tackle the challenges posed by burgeoning user demands and system loads. Load balancing bolsters resilience, caching accelerates data access, and database optimization refines query execution – collectively shaping an ecosystem that thrives on performance. As you navigate the intricate domains of load balancing configurations, caching methodologies, and database enhancements, you steer your application toward a realm where speed, scalability, and dependability intersect to deliver extraordinary user experiences.

Handling database sharding and horizontal scaling

Within the expansive realm of architecting applications to gracefully tackle the formidable challenges posed by immense data growth and surging user demands, the adept management of database sharding and horizontal scaling stands as a critical prowess. As the digital horizon continues its dynamic evolution, databases find themselves tasked with the mission of efficiently managing ever-expanding volumes of data while upholding impeccable performance standards. In this discourse, we embark on a voyage to explore the intricacies of database sharding and horizontal scaling, unraveling their paramount significance and delving into the intricate technical facets of their seamless integration.

Revealing the Nuances of Database Sharding and Horizontal Scaling

Database Sharding materializes as a technique wherein vast datasets are thoughtfully partitioned into more manageable subsets referred to as shards. Each distinct shard is then allocated to a dedicated database instance, orchestrating the distribution of data across multiple servers. This methodology bears fruits in the realms of data distribution, parallelism, and sets the stage for accommodating future data expansion.

Horizontal Scaling, in contrast, encompasses the expansion of an application's capabilities through the strategic addition of more servers or nodes to the infrastructure. This paradigm empowers applications to navigate increased user traffic and grapple with soaring data volumes by distributing the workload across a constellation of resources.

Code Example: Unveiling the Mechanics of Database Sharding

Here, we present an illustrative example demonstrating how database sharding can be elegantly accomplished within a Django framework:

python

```
class ShardedProduct(models.Model):
    shard_id = models.IntegerField()
    name = models.CharField(max_length=100)
    price = models.DecimalField(max_digits=10,
decimal_places=2)

    class Meta:
        unique_together = ('shard_id', 'id')
```

Navigating the Complex Tapestry of Database Sharding

Database sharding entails an intricate web of implications spanning application architecture and the meticulous choreography of data management. This endeavor necessitates a keen understanding of the art of partitioning data across shards, the artful selection of the sharding key, and the mechanics of adroitly routing queries to their designated shard. When executed thoughtfully, sharding can yield exponential improvements in query performance as queries are distributed in parallel across the array of shards.

Horizontal Scaling: Orchestrating the Symphony of Enhanced Performance

Horizontal scaling functions on the foundational premise that the infusion of additional resources corresponds to a linear amplification in both performance and capacity. This approach involves the strategic addition of more servers to the infrastructure, a feat often facilitated by load balancers adeptly orchestrating the uniform distribution of incoming requests among the diverse nodes.

Code Example: Configuring Load Balancing

Behold a concise code snippet shedding light on a straightforward configuration of load balancing through the utilization of NGINX:

nginx

```
http {
    upstream app_servers {
        server server1;
        server server2;
        # Include additional server instances as deemed
requisite
    }

    server {
        listen 80;
        server_name example.com;

        location / {
            proxy_pass http://app_servers;
        }
    }
}
```

Striking the Harmonious Balance: Crafting for Triumph

The seamless integration of database sharding and horizontal scaling mandates a delicate equilibrium between the advantages they bestow and the intricacies they introduce. Gaining a profound understanding of the application's unique data access patterns, the nuanced behavior of queries, and the trajectory of anticipated growth is of the essence. Furthermore, meticulous charting of sharding strategies, the discerning selection of apt sharding keys, and the architecting of an effortless mechanism for query routing collectively form the bedrock of this mastery.

Within the ever-evolving panorama of web application craftsmanship, the adept navigation of database sharding and horizontal scaling unfurls as a pivotal art. These techniques stand as quintessential pillars to fortify applications against the tides of burgeoning data loads and soaring user requisites, ensuring they not only endure but flourish. As you venture into the labyrinthine world of database sharding, assimilating its intricate tapestry and seamlessly aligning it with the idiosyncrasies of your application's demands will forge a path toward a more resilient and scalable data architecture. When harmoniously coupled with horizontal scaling, this journey culminates in an application ecosystem primed to elegantly traverse the multifaceted landscapes of contemporary data-driven challenges with adeptness and excellence.

Chapter Ten

Optimizing Django Application Performance

Profiling Django applications and identifying bottlenecks

In the realm of crafting supremely efficient Django applications, the intricacies of profiling and uncovering bottlenecks emerge as critical crafts. Profiling entails the methodical exploration of an application's performance nuances, guiding developers to spotlight resource-intensive code segments and illuminate avenues for enhancement. In this exploration, we embark on an odyssey through the intricacies of profiling Django applications, casting light on its pivotal importance and delving into the methodologies and tools that empower the identification of performance bottlenecks.

The Core of Profiling

The essence of profiling resides in systematically discerning an application's runtime behavior and resource employment. This encompasses a spectrum of strategies aimed at capturing insights into CPU utilization, memory allocation, database queries, and interactions with external services. Profiling arms developers with empirical data, grounding performance assumptions and paving a path toward precision-driven optimizations.

Techniques for Profiling Django Applications

1. Manual Profiling:

Manual profiling entails judiciously embedding timing code snippets within critical junctures of your application's codebase. By gauging the time consumed by specific code segments, developers can unveil performance incongruities and pinpoint prospective bottlenecks.

2. Django Debug Toolbar:

The Django Debug Toolbar stands as a potent asset for profiling applications during development. This interactive panel seamlessly integrates into the Django admin interface, delivering real-time glimpses into database queries, cache utilization, and more. Scrutinizing query counts and durations furnishes developers with visibility into latent inefficiencies.

3. Python Profilers:

Python extends built-in profiling modules such as cProfile and profile, generating comprehensive reports that chronicle the execution duration of each function within an application. These profilers come to the fore when assessing the performance of individual views, methods, or functions.

4. Third-Party Profilers:

Third-party profilers like Pyflame and Py-Spy plunge deeper into application execution, permitting the exploration of CPU consumption and thread behavior. These profilers prove invaluable for unveiling bottlenecks in multi-threaded or asynchronous applications.

Code Illustration: Embarking on Manual Profiling

python

```
import time

def resource_intensive_function():
    start_time = time.time()

    # Code representing a task demanding resources

    end_time = time.time()
    elapsed_time = end_time - start_time
    print(f"Time taken: {elapsed_time} seconds")
```

Unveiling Bottleneck Triggers: A Strategic Stance

1. Database Queries: Probe the frequency of queries executed per request and their durations. Streamline by harnessing database indexes, curbing redundant queries, and embracing Django ORM's select_related and prefetch_related optimizations.

2. View Performance: Gauge the execution duration of views. Contemplate the application of Django's inbuilt caching mechanisms, curbing the number of database queries, and embracing asynchronous programming where fitting.

3. Memory Utilization: Monitor memory consumption using tools like memory_profiler. Discern memory leaks, fine-tune memory-intensive operations, and assure efficient resource allocation.

4. External Service Calls: Scrutinize interactions with external APIs or services. Integrate caching for API responses, tap into asynchronous programming for non-blocking requests, and entertain rate limiting to forestall overwhelming external services.

Profiling Django applications emerges as a compass on the journey of performance optimization. Through avenues like manual profiling, the embrace of tools like Django Debug Toolbar and Python profilers, and the sagacious identification of bottlenecks, developers unlock newfound dimensions of application efficiency. Profiling bestows the gift of informed decision-making, steering optimizations that guarantee applications don't just meet performance expectations but transcend them. As the digital terrain evolves, the finesse in profiling becomes an unwavering asset in the arsenal of any developer seeking to deliver top-tier, high-performance Django marvels.

Performance tuning using caching, asynchronous tasks, and database optimization

In the realm of crafting impeccably performing Django applications, the harmonious interplay of caching, asynchronous tasks, and database optimization stands as a symphony of strategies that compose the art of optimization. Performance tuning, the craft of refining an application's efficiency and responsiveness, finds its essence in these techniques. In this exploration, we embark on a journey through the intricacies of performance enhancement, exploring the significance of caching, asynchronous tasks, and database optimization. We delve into the methodologies and tools that empower developers to achieve peak performance, painting a picture of performance excellence.

Unleashing the Power of Caching

Caching, a fundamental cornerstone of performance optimization, revolves around the strategic storage of frequently accessed data. This practice expedites data retrieval and alleviates server processing, leading to streamlined resource utilization and accelerated response times. Caching strategies span a spectrum from page-level caching to object caching, each tailored to the nuances of an application's requirements.

Leveraging the Strength of Page-Level Caching

Page-level caching, often facilitated by frameworks like Django's built-in caching, preserves entire HTML pages. This empowers servers to promptly deliver pre-rendered pages, obviating the need for repetitive resource-intensive rendering processes.

Implementing the Precision of Object Caching

Object caching, on the other hand, homes in on frequently accessed data from the database or results of intricate computations. Storing such data in a cache enables subsequent requests to be promptly satisfied from the cache, bypassing the need for redundant database queries or computations and significantly enhancing response times.

Code Example: Employing Django's Caching Framework

python

```python
from django.core.cache import cache

def get_data_from_cache_or_db():
    data = cache.get('cached_data')
    if data is None:
        data = fetch_data_from_database()
        cache.set('cached_data', data, timeout=3600)  #
Cache for an hour
    return data
```

Navigating the Agile Landscape with Asynchronous Tasks

Asynchronous programming assumes a central role in the performance enhancement saga. This methodology disentangles tasks from the synchronous request-response cycle, facilitating non-blocking execution of resource-intensive operations. Asynchronous tasks find their forte in managing I/O-bound operations, such as database queries, external API calls, and file operations.

Crafting the Symphony of Asynchronous Views and Tasks

Django's asynchronous views and the versatile asyncio framework serve as potent tools for managing asynchronous tasks. These tasks enable the parallel execution of time-intensive operations, ensuring the application maintains responsiveness while optimally utilizing resources.

Code Example: An Asynchronous View in Django

python

```
from django.http import JsonResponse
from asgiref.sync import async_to_sync
import asyncio

@async_to_sync
async def asynchronous_view(request):
    # Simulating an asynchronous task
    await asyncio.sleep(2)
    return JsonResponse({'message': 'Task completed'})
```

Elevating the Database Performance through Precision Optimization

Database optimization emerges as a keystone in the pursuit of high-performance applications. A finely tuned database can wield a considerable impact on query execution times, scalability, and the overall speed of the application. Strategies encompass indexing, query optimization, database normalization, and, in specific scenarios, denormalization to balance read and write operations.

Tapping into the Power of Indexing

Database indexing entails the creation of data structures that expedite data retrieval operations. By employing indexes on frequently queried columns, the data retrieval process is accelerated by reducing the number of records that require scanning.

Code Example: Implementing Database Indexing in Django Models

python

```
class Product(models.Model):
    name = models.CharField(max_length=100,
```

```
db_index=True)
    category = models.ForeignKey(Category,
on_delete=models.CASCADE, db_index=True)
    price = models.DecimalField(max_digits=10,
decimal_places=2)
```

Navigating the Path of Performance Excellence

Caching, asynchronous tasks, and database optimization intertwine harmoniously to shape the fabric of performance tuning. While each technique contributes uniquely to the optimization landscape, their fusion is the key. Caching expedites data retrieval, asynchronous tasks unlock agility, and database optimization propels enhanced query execution and data access.

The voyage toward crafting Django applications of peak performance finds its guiding stars in caching, asynchronous tasks, and database optimization. The strategic deployment of caching strategies, the artful mastery of asynchronous programming, and the finesse of database optimization collectively fuel an application ecosystem that not only meets performance standards but transcends them. In a dynamic digital landscape, the adeptness in these techniques becomes a formidable asset, empowering developers to engineer solutions that fluidly waltz to the rhythm of performance excellence.

Utilizing CDN and edge caching for faster content delivery

Navigating the Path of Content Delivery Mastery

In the realm of optimizing web applications, the strategic orchestration of Content Delivery Networks (CDNs) and the finesse of edge caching emerge as an artful dance that ushers in unparalleled content delivery speeds. As our digital landscape continues to evolve, user expectations for rapid and seamless content access soar to new heights. In this exploration, we embark on a journey through the intricacies of leveraging CDNs and edge caching to achieve nimble content delivery. We decipher their importance, delve into the mechanics, and explore how these techniques interlace to revolutionize the user experience.

Grasping the Core of CDNs and Edge Caching

Content Delivery Networks (CDNs) materialize as networks of servers dispersed across the globe, thoughtfully positioned at diverse geographic points. The primary goal of a CDN is to expedite web content delivery by relying on the nearest server to the user. This approach mitigates latency caused by data traversing long distances, resulting in swift load times and an elevated user experience.

Edge caching is a pivotal facet of CDNs. It encompasses the caching of frequently accessed content on the "edge" servers, situated closest to the user. Through this caching strategy, content can be swiftly delivered to users, virtually eliminating latency.

Tracing the Journey of Content via CDNs

1. Replicating Content: Upon integration with a CDN, web content is meticulously duplicated across multiple servers within the CDN network. This replication process ensures that content is readily accessible across servers dispersed in various global regions.

2. Proximity-Driven Delivery: When a user seeks content, the CDN shrewdly directs the request to the server closest to the user's location. This proximity-driven approach drastically curtails the time needed to fetch and deliver the content.

3. Edge Cache Enlightenment: As users access content, the CDN's edge servers cache frequently requested files. Subsequent appeals for the same content are fulfilled from these edge caches, effectively minimizing the necessity to retrieve content from the origin server.

The Merits of Employing CDNs and Edge Caching

1. Latency Reduction: Through content delivery from servers situated in close proximity to users, CDNs and edge caching profoundly diminish latency. This outcome translates to expedited load times and an enhanced user experience.

2. Scalability Edge: CDNs shine when traffic spikes transpire, as they proficiently distribute the load across their array of servers. This scalability assurance guarantees an application's responsiveness even amid surges in traffic.

3. Bandwidth Savvy: With edge caching in play, the burden on the origin server is lightened, thanks to the delivery of frequently accessed content from edge servers. This dynamic leads to economical bandwidth usage and optimized resource allocation.

4. Global Accessibililty: CDNs stretch their wings across the globe, ensuring that users across various geographical domains access content speedily, unaffected by server distances.

Code Illustration: Integrating Django with a CDN

Seamlessly integrating a CDN with Django can be executed through tools like django-storages. The ensuing example showcases integration with Amazon S3 for the purpose of utilizing a CDN to serve static and media files.

python

```python
# settings.py
AWS_STORAGE_BUCKET_NAME = 'your-bucket-name'
AWS_S3_CUSTOM_DOMAIN =
f'{AWS_STORAGE_BUCKET_NAME}.s3.amazonaws.com'
AWS_S3_OBJECT_PARAMETERS = {
    'CacheControl': 'max-age=86400',  # Cache files for
a day
}
STATIC_URL = f'https://{AWS_S3_CUSTOM_DOMAIN}/static/'
MEDIA_URL = f'https://{AWS_S3_CUSTOM_DOMAIN}/media/'
```

Elevating the User Experience through Strategic Caching

CDNs and edge caching join hands to gift users an experience infused with seamless brilliance. By expeditiously delivering content from edge servers in proximity to users and minimizing data traversal distances, these techniques wield the transformative power to redefine load times and overall performance. As the digital terrain unfurls, the synergy between CDNs and the artistry of edge caching asserts itself as a quintessential bridge between user aspirations and the reality of web application performance.

In the symphony of web application optimization, CDNs and edge caching step forward as virtuoso performers that orchestrate swifter content delivery. The dexterous utilization of CDNs enriches global reach, diminishes latency, and maximizes resource allocation. Paired with the prowess of edge caching, which positions frequently accessed content at users' fingertips, the outcome is an ecosystem that thrives on speed and responsiveness. As developers navigate the ever-evolving digital panorama, mastery of these techniques transforms into a prized asset, ensuring that applications resonate harmoniously with the clamor for quicker, smoother, and more efficient content delivery.

Conclusion

Reflecting on the journey to Django mastery

As we journey through the realms of Django development, a moment of introspection beckons – an opportunity to reflect on the path that leads to mastery in this intricate web framework. This juncture invites us to delve into the evolving landscape of skills, insights, and accomplishments that shape the odyssey to becoming an adept Django developer. In this discussion, we unravel the significance of pausing to reflect on this journey, uncovering the milestones, challenges, and transformations that pave the way towards achieving expertise.

Navigating the Progression Landscape

The expedition towards Django mastery encompasses more than just technical prowess; it entails an amalgamation of theory, hands-on experience, and a profound grasp of the Django ecosystem. Each developer embarking on this quest charts their own course, navigating through distinct phases – from the tentative first steps into Django's realm to the confident strides of crafting sophisticated applications.

Tracing the Markers of Progress

**1. **Inaugural Encounter: **The journey embarks with acquainting oneself with Django's fundamental components, comprehending its architecture, and gaining proficiency in building views, models, and templates. These foundational steps lay the groundwork for all subsequent endeavors.

**2. **Architectural Insight: **As the expedition unfolds, a deeper understanding of architectural paradigms emerges. Developers become adept at constructing modular applications, implementing reusable elements, and grasping the intricacies of Object-Relational Mapping (ORM).

**3. **Venturing into Advanced Territories: **The journey then propels forward into advanced domains such as authentication mechanisms, building APIs, delving into asynchronous programming, and honing skills in performance optimization. These facets contribute to rounding off a skilled Django developer's toolkit.

**4. **Incorporating Prudent Practices: **Throughout the journey, the assimilation of best practices assumes paramount importance. This includes adhering to the tenet of "Don't Repeat Yourself" (DRY), crafting code that is both clean and maintainable, and employing design patterns that resonate harmoniously with Django's philosophy.

Tackling Challenges as Stepping Stones

**1. **The Learning Curve: **The initial stages of the journey might present a steep learning curve. Gaining an understanding of the Django paradigm and navigating its intricate ecosystem demands patience, determination, and an insatiable hunger for knowledge.

**2. **Grasping Complex Advanced Concepts: **Navigating the domain of advanced concepts, including asynchronous programming, optimization strategies, and intricate database management, can prove to be a formidable challenge. Yet, these challenges are stepping stones to growth and mastery.

**3. **Adapting to Dynamic Technological Shifts: **The Django landscape is characterized by constant evolution – new versions, features, and technologies are frequently introduced. Developers traversing this journey must be prepared to adapt to these shifts, embracing continuous learning to stay updated.

Embracing Transformations: The Emergence of a Maestro

The expedition towards Django mastery isn't solely about acquiring technical skills; it's a metamorphosis. It's the evolution from a novice developer to a skilled artisan capable of architecting intricate applications, optimizing performance, and delivering solutions that embody best practices.

The Ripple Effect of Mastery

Attaining mastery in Django reverberates beyond individual skills; it resonates within the projects created. Accomplished developers engineer applications with scalability, maintainability, and efficiency as guiding principles. Their codebase exudes elegance, their solutions are marked by ingenuity, and they contribute to the broader Django community through open-source projects, forums, and mentorship.

Stopping to reflect on the travel towards Django mastery is an work out in recognizing the advancement of aptitudes, surmounting challenges, and grasping change. It's a tribute to the endless hours contributed in learning, coding, and problem-solving. It's a celebration of advance, versatility, and the faithful commitment to ceaseless development. As we take this minute of reflection, we not as it were honor our individual journey but moreover set the course for the another stage of our travel – one that dives more profound into the domain of conceivable outcomes that Django mastery unfurls.

Emphasizing the importance of clean and correct code in building professional-grade solutions

Within the pages of this volume, we have traversed the intricacies of Django, unearthing its architecture, mastering its functionalities, and harnessing its potential to fashion web solutions of a professional caliber. From the complexities of advanced project configuration and customizable admin interfaces to the realm of real-time functionalities, caching intricacies, and the art of crafting scalable architecture, our expedition through Django's universe has been all-encompassing.

We've dug profound into the domains of APIs, asynchronous programming, look optimization, and the science of refining execution. The acknowledgment of the significance of perfect and exact code has been an basic subject that reverberates all through our travel, shaping the bedrock of our interest of fabulousness in program craftsmanship.

As we bring this journey to a conclusion, it's an fortunate minute to reflect on the transformative voyage we've embraced. Our advancement from learners to proficient specialists, from novices to modelers of complicated applications, has been nothing brief of momentous. The travel to achieve authority in Django has unfurled not as it were as a voyage into specialized ability but too as a confirmation to our constant commitment to development and learning.

As we part ways with these pages, let us carry forth the wisdom accrued, the skills honed, and the insights gleaned. The realm of Django and web development is in perpetual flux, demanding a perpetual commitment to staying abreast of advancements and embracing innovation. Equipped with the knowledge distilled within these chapters, we stand prepared to traverse the ever-evolving landscape of technology and to craft solutions that make a profound impact.

In conclusion, let us weave into our ethos the principles of immaculate code, precision, and creative thought. Let us press forward, continuously refining our craft, elevating our endeavors, and contributing to the vibrant and dynamic Django community. This book doesn't signify a terminus but rather an inception – an opening to ascend even higher in the realm of web solutions of professional stature.